Physical Characteristics of the English Toy Spaniel

(from the American Kennel Club breed standard)

D1408772

Topline: Level.

Body: Short, compact, square and deep.

Tail: Docked to 2 to 4 inches in length.

Hindquarters: Rear legs are well muscled and nicely angulated to indicate strength, and parallel of hock.

Feet: Front and rear, are neat and compact.

Size: The most desirable weight of an adult is 8 to 14 pounds.

English Toy Spaniel

By Lee Sherwin

9   **History of the** English Toy Spaniel

Uncover the aristocratic background of the English Toy Spaniel by discussing the origins of the toy spaniels and learning how the breed became established in England, its homeland. Follow the breed across the Atlantic and trace its history in the US.

25   **Characteristics of the** English Toy Spaniel

With a regal beauty befitting its native country, the English Toy Spaniel is an affectionate companion in a compact size that can fit in most anywhere. Small in stature yet big in personality, the English Toy Spaniel is a true charmer! Topics include the breed's temperament, owner suitablity and potential health problems in the breed.

30   **Breed Standard for the** English Toy Spaniel

Learn the requirements of a well-bred English Toy Spaniel by studying the description of the breed set forth in the American Kennel Club standard. Both show dogs and pets must possess key characteristics as outlined in the breed standard.

37   **Your Puppy** English Toy Spaniel

Find out about how to locate a well-bred English Toy Spaniel puppy. Discover which questions to ask the breeder and what to expect when visiting the litter. Prepare for your puppy-accessory shopping spree. Also discussed are home safety, the first trip to the vet, socialization and solving basic puppy problems.

61   **Proper Care of Your** English Toy Spaniel

Cover the specifics of taking care of your English Toy Spaniel every day: feeding for the puppy, adult and senior dog; grooming, including coat care, ears, eyes, nails and bathing; and exercise needs for your dog. Also discussed are the essentials of dog identification.

78   **Training Your** English Toy Spaniel

Begin with the basics of training the puppy and adult dog. Learn the principles of house-training the English Toy Spaniel, including the use of crates and basic scent instincts. Get started by introducing the pup to his collar and leash and progress to the basic commands. Find out about obedience classes and other activities.

Contents

Healthcare of Your English Toy Spaniel   **103**

By Lowell Ackerman DVM, DACVD
Become your dog's healthcare advocate and a well-educated canine keeper. Select a skilled and able veterinarian. Discuss pet insurance, vaccinations and infectious diseases, the neuter/spay decision and a sensible, effective plan for parasite control, including fleas, ticks and worms.

Your Senior English Toy Spaniel   **126**

Know when to consider your English Toy Spaniel a senior and what special needs he will have. Learn to recognize the signs of aging in terms of physical and behavioral traits and what your vet can do to optimize your dog's golden years. Consider some advice about saying goodbye to your beloved pet.

Showing Your English Toy Spaniel   **135**

Step into the center ring and find out about the world of showing pure-bred dogs. Here's a basic overview of ACK conformation showing, including how to get started and what's required for your dog to become a champion. Take a leap into the realms of obedience trials, rally obedience and agility.

Behavior of Your English Toy Spaniel   **145**

Analyze the canine mind to understand what makes your English Toy Spaniel tick. The following potential problems are addressed: separation anxiety, sexual misconduct, chewing, digging, barking and food-related problems.

KENNEL CLUB BOOKS® **ENGLISH TOY SPANIEL**
ISBN: 1-59378-332-9

Copyright © 2007 • Kennel Club Books® • A Division of BowTie, Inc.
40 Broad Street, Freehold, NJ 07728 USA
Cover Design Patented: US 6,435,559 B2 • Printed in South Korea

Library of Congress Cataloging-in-Publication Data
Sherwin, Lee.
English toy spaniel / by Lee Sherwin.
p. cm.
1. English toy spaniel. I. Title.
SF429.E73S54 2007
636.76—dc22
2006016291

10 9 8 7 6 5 4 3 2 1

Photography by Carol Ann Johnson
with additional photographs by:

Ashbey Photography, Norvia Behling, Mary Bloom, Booth Photography, Paulette Braun, Carolina Biological Supply, David Dalton, Isabelle Français, Bill Jonas, Kohler Studios, Dr. Dennis Kunkel, Tam C. Nguyen, Phototake, Jean Claude Revy, Susan & Lennah Studios, Chuck Tatham, Alice van Kempen and Missy Yuhl.

Illustrations by Patricia Peters.

The publisher wishes to thank all of the owners whose dogs are illustrated in this book, including Michael Allen, Mea Askins, Debi Bell-Dolan, Mark Dolan, Jerome Elliott, Wendy Goddyn, Bonnie J. Miller, DVM, Karen Miller, Thomas O'Neal, Jussi Palosaari, F. & K. Pounder, M. & R. Shannon, Vanessa Weber, Caleb M. Williams, John Wood and Eugene Zaphiris.

The English Toy Spaniel is a true combination of beauty, dignity and personality. Known as a toy dog throughout the world, this diminutive spaniel with an aristocratic past is a popular and charming companion.

ENGLISH TOY SPANIEL

A toy dog through and through, the English Toy Spaniel is classified in the Toy Group of breeds in the UK and on the Continent as well as in the US and Canada. While in North America he is known as the English Toy Spaniel, in the UK and Europe he is known as the King Charles Spaniel. Whatever his name, this is a delightful toy spaniel from England to whom we will refer in this book as the English Toy Spaniel.

Working dogs have been around for centuries, bred to assist humans with various jobs and chores. The pastoral dogs would herd and guard the sheep and cattle, and the hounds coursed after deer, rabbits or whatever could be put upon man's table for a meal. The terriers, large and small, evolved into fast, spirited dogs who could rid a farm of foxes, woodchucks and badgers and who could rid a home of rodents and vermin. The gundogs evolved early on to assist the hunter in bringing home his quarry for the family's table. All of these dogs had a purpose and were bred to make humans' lives easier. The dogs that were unable to do the job for

An early illustration of "Blenheim Spaniels." Bred and kept by the Duke of Marlborough, the chestnut and white variety was named for his family's place of residence, Blenheim Palace.

ABOUT OUR BREED'S NAMESAKE

The interests of King Charles II included the theater, gambling and horseracing. His court was worldly and extravagant, and there was no secret about his many mistresses or the rumored 17 children that he had by them.

which they were bred were disposed of, and those who could do a good day's work were bred.

Over the generations, talents and abilities were honed and perfected: the dogs became keener of eyesight and scent, swifter of leg and quicker at the hunt. These were the dogs that lived and worked side by side with man, becoming part of his workforce but not always members of his family.

Toy dogs have been around for centuries as well, belonging to the aristocrats and the royalty, whether in England, France, China or Egypt. Dr. Johannes Caius wrote in *Of English Dogs*, written in Latin in 1536, "These dogs are little, pretty and fine, and sought for to satisfy the delicateness of dainty dames and wanton women's wills, instruments of folly for them to play

Champions of the 1930s, left to right: Eng. Ch. Ashton-More Domino, Eng. Ch. Cystal, Eng. Ch. Ashton-More Crusader, Eng. Ch. Ashton-More Wildflower and Eng. Ch. Barritone.

From the early 1930s, this illustration was reproduced from a pastel drawing specially made for *Hutchinson's Dog Encyclopaedia* by the famous animal artist Mrs. G. Shaw-Baker. Shown are the Blenheim and Prince Charles varieties of the English Toy Spaniel.

and dally with, to trifle away the treasure of time. These puppies, the smaller they be, the more pleasure they provoke, as more meet playfellows for mincing mistresses to bear in their bosoms."

As civilization advanced, man realized that dogs could be bred for pleasure as well as for work, and, as the Industrial Revolution began to lighten man's workload, he had more of an inclination to

COMFORTERS AND FLEA TRAPS

The toy dogs were sometimes called "Comforter" dogs. In the 16th and 17th centuries, bathing was not done on a regular basis and personal hygiene was poor compared to modern standards. Dogs were often held on laps with the thought that the dog would become host to the fleas that were on the mistress or master. These dogs were also referred to as "living flea traps." In addition, the dogs were used for warmth in the drafty palaces and mansions.

Two English Toy Spaniels owned by Mrs. A. H. Bradley were among the participants in the Ladies' Kennel Club show of May 1931, held in Olympia, England.

Eng. Ch. Ashton-More Baronet, bred by Mr. F. G. Borryer, was exhibited in the early 20th century and was an important sire.

bring the dog inside and to make it his companion. For the lofty role of companion dog, it was difficult to find a better pet than a toy dog. With the toys, one would have the choice of a smooth or long coat, a long or cobby body, a pushed-in or elongated muzzle and short or long legs. Whatever the toy dogs' physical construction, they all have affectionate natures and a longing to be close

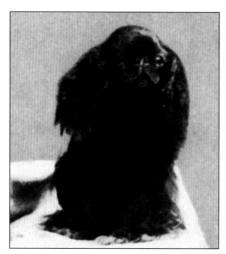

Born in 1927, Eng. Ch. Ashton-More Nebo won his first Challenge Certificate in 1929. He weighed 9.5 pounds and is considered to be exemplary of breed type at that time.

to their masters or mistresses.

Because of the diminutive size of these dogs, few weighing much over 10 pounds, the toys have been referred to by big-dog owners as fops, mutants and neurotics, and their owners were thought to be individuals who only liked to sit around with a dog up their sleeves or on their laps. On the contrary, although most toy dogs like to sit on or

'TIL DEATH DO US PART

Mary, Queen of Scots was said to have had a small dog hiding in her skirts at the time of her execution. When discovered later, the dog was covered with his mistress's blood.

When Charles I was put to death, a spaniel walked beside him to the place of his execution and the little dog was put on display that night by the soldiers.

near their masters or mistresses, they can be tough little tykes who can stand their ground, take a good walk through the park or jump the hoops in agility or the hurdles in obedience, just like the big dogs. The toy dogs, whether it be the Maltese in his glorious white coat, the Yorkshire Terrier with his steel-gray flowing coat, the English Toy Spaniel with his glorious colors and "pug" face or any of the other delightful small breeds, all are great pets and

A drawing from around the turn of the 20th century of "Lord Tennyson," a noted winner of his time.

highly competitive in the Best in Show ring.

The toy spaniel was originally believed to have come from the Far East, specifically China or Japan. The pushed-in nose and the protruding eyes are reminiscent of the very old Eastern breeds, the Pekingese and the Japanese Chin. Some thought has been given to the possibility of the dog's originally having come from Spain, the home of the "spaniels," and then arriving in the East, where eventually it was exported to England via Holland or France. There is a possibility that Captain Saris, a British naval officer, took a pair of dogs back to England with him in the early 1600s as a gift for King James I from the Japanese Emperor, as the Japanese always included dogs with their royal presents.

The history of these wonderful little spaniels has been recorded quite well in England through the work of superb portraitists, especially Van Dyck's paintings in the

THE KING SPEAKS

In 1903, King Charles fanciers tried to change the name of the breed to the Toy Spaniel but King Edward VII, an ardent supporter of the breed, objected to the name change. Thus the breed in the United Kingdom has remained the King Charles Spaniel.

Some believe that the toy spaniel originated with dogs from the Far East. The face and eyes of the Pekingese, shown here, certainly bear resemblance to those of the English Toy.

The Pug, shown here, was also popular with royalty in the early days of the English Toy Spaniel.

17th century. The dogs often were pictured with both King Charles I and King Charles II, thus becoming known as the King Charles Spaniel, even though the dog had been known in England since the 1500s. The spaniel remained very popular with the royals through the reign of James II and it was also popular in France during the reign of Henry III. With the fall of the house of Stuart, the English Toy Spaniel lost its place of favor, as William and Mary preferred the other popular toy, the Pug.

The original English Toy Spaniels were only black and tan in color, with the other three color varieties being developed at later times. Some confusion about the dogs developed over the years because of the different names that were given to the various color combinations. Although the toy spaniels were all of the same type, different names were given to each classification of coat color. The original black and tan variety was called King Charles, the solid red coloration was called Ruby, the tricolor pattern was called Prince Charles and the chestnut and white pattern was called Blenheim. These names are still applied to the colors, though all varieties are regarded as English Toy Spaniels and shown in the same classes at shows. The King Charles and Ruby varieties are considered whole colors, while the Blenheim and Prince Charles

The original English Toy Spaniel was the black and tan; at one time no other colors existed. Thus the black and tan variety has retained the name "King Charles," as the breed is known as the King Charles Spaniel in its homeland.

are parti-colors, as they have white in their coats.

The English Toy Spaniel, although primarily a companion dog, originally was used as a hunting dog, as were all of the other, larger, spaniels. John Churchill, the first Duke of Marlborough, was an avid fancier and used his dogs for hunting woodcocks and other small game birds. The use of these small dogs for hunting waned, as the dogs tired quickly. The larger spaniels took over from the small dogs, as they were able to work a whole day in the field alongside their masters.

The Duke bred the chestnut and white spaniels, thus the name Blenheim, for the family's residence. At Blenheim Palace can be

FOUR COLOR VARIETIES
King Charles—Black and tan.
Ruby—Red.
Prince Charles—Tricolor.
Blenheim—Chestnut and white.

In 1932, the four varieties were classified as King Charles Spaniels and have remained such in Europe. Will Judy, in the *Dog Encyclopaedia*, noted that "Where there are color classifications, the quality suffers because breeders seek color rather than quality." Freeman Lloyd opines, "Fashions in toy dogs change almost as often as styles in dress!"

seen a portrait by Sir Godfrey Kneller, picturing the small chestnut and white spaniels at the feet or in the laps of the women. It was said that the Duke acquired his first pair of spaniels from China. The Blenheim spaniels were bred by the Marlborough Dukes for years, and they were considered to be the best and the smallest of the toy spaniels.

The toy spaniel always has been a popular toy dog in England. By 1861, classes for toy dogs were held at the Birmingham dog show, two years after the first classes were held for gundogs. In 1885, the Toy Spaniel Club was formed, and the dogs were divided by color and a standard for the breed was drafted. It called for a compact and cobby body with a wide and deep chest, a well-domed head, a massive skull, a short nose and a deep stop. The dog was to have a long, straight and silky coat with heavy feathering on the legs, ears and tail. The standard has changed very little over the years, except to clarify certain points. In 1923, the colors were reclassified under one breed name and, since that time, all

colors have competed together for the Best of Breed award.

Queen Victoria also was an ardent admirer of the breed and owned a spaniel called Dash. Another dog, Darmail Wild, won over 100 first places at shows during Victorian times.

The Cavalier King Charles Spaniel is a separate breed with a very similar history. The Cavalier originally was classified with the toy spaniels. In 1928, it became a breed of its own and its name changed to the Cavalier. The Cavalier is a larger and heavier dog than the English Toy Spaniel, longer in foreface and with a jaw more like that of the Cocker

A LASTING IMPRINT: THE THUMB MARK

The Blenheim (red and white) has the much desired "thumb mark" on its forehead. Legend has it that while the Duke was in battle, his wife Sarah sat with a spaniel bitch, who was in whelp, on her lap. In her nervousness, the Duchess pressed her thumb on the bitch's head and when the puppies were whelped, all had a chestnut-colored spot on their foreheads the size of a thumb.

THE OTHER TOY SPANIEL

When distinguishing between the English Toy Spaniel and the Cavalier King Charles Spaniel, remember that the English Toy Spaniel has the shorter muzzle and thus the shorter name! But also remember that the Cavalier is a larger dog (13–18 lbs) than the English Toy, whose weight runs between 8–14 lbs. Both breeds have the same color combinations, but the English Toy has the Pug-type muzzle.

Spaniel than the Pekingese.

In 1930, Will Judy wrote, "Perhaps the epitaph of the breed was first written when the fad for short noses pushed-up between the eyes became the 'go' of the breeders. Then, the breed lost its resemblance to the general spaniel family. Here is the case of a worthy small dog that finds its worst enemy in its supposed friends, its breeder." Mr. Judy's prediction certainly has proven worthless. In the 21st century, the English Toy Spaniel remains a beloved pure-bred dog with a steady following around the world.

THE ENGLISH TOY SPANIEL IN THE US

by Michael Allen
These highly valued toy dogs made the perilous journey across the sea to America in company of the jewels and treasures of the wealthy and, being a hardy strain, they flourished in their new home. Even the *Mayflower* was reputed to have listed "Spanyls" on their manifest. Despite their role as an adornment for those desirous of having a cheerful, devoted and distinctive companion, the breed was reputed to be a keen little hunting dog, especially on the diminutive woodcock that abounded in this new land.

The English Toy Spaniel has enjoyed registration with the American Kennel Club (AKC) since 1886, appearing in their records since the club was founded. The first of the breed to be recorded was Mildmay Park Beauty in that year, and the registration number was 4456. Prior to 1903 all four colors were

Displaying red and white coloration are an English Toy Spaniel and a Cavalier King Charles Spaniel.

designated as separate breeds for the purposes of showing and allowed to mingle for breeding, but the following year the AKC decreed they would be one breed and would be exhibited in the four color varieties that are seen today. The official written standard for the breed was first approved in 1909, with subsequent revisions in 1959 and 1989.

The first English Toy Spaniel exhibited at Westminster Kennel Club was in 1877, and since that time only five have achieved placement in the Toy Group since group competition was originally offered in 1924. The first was a Blenheim and Prince Charles in 1935 and the last was a King Charles and Ruby in 1984.

While the breed enjoyed great popularity in the 1890s and the early years of the 1900s, such popularity faded in favor of other toy breeds until the 1930s when it virtually disappeared. After World War II a handful of dedicated breeders made diligent efforts, and the breed began a slow and painstaking revival until the 21st century. Individual registrations reached 256 out of 144 litters in the year 2005. From this number, 52 of these unique little dogs achieved AKC championships.

In the early days several breeders' efforts to resurrect the breed greatly improved the situation. One noted prefix was Virginia Paine's Vica. She bred a Ruby dog, Ch. Vica Cardinal, who won the Group at the huge Trenton show in the 1960s and was one of the first to achieve such an award. Other noted prefixes that may be found in pedigrees but have passed on into history are Tarahall, Esadale, Marsy, Celamo, An'dor, Cedar Crest, Jekada, Jaor, Esadale, Veldale and Godric. We cannot forget the Locksley Hall Charlies of the late Thomas Conway, who began breeding in 1948, eventually becoming a multiple group judge but, until his death, remaining a staunch advocate for the English Toy Spaniel. He imported Ch. Kirklyn Jeeves of Maibee from the noted British breeder of both Charlies and Cavaliers, Sheila Waters, but in turn sold him to Christine Thaxton of Kings Court. The first English Toy to earn the prestigious Phillips System All-Time Top Producer Award was Locksley Hall Trooper, bred by Mr. Conway.

In 1959 the venerable Ab Sidewater of *Popular Dogs*, the first publication to receive the Outstanding All-breed Dog Publication award from the Dog Writers Association of America, published *The Visualizations of the Dog Standards*, an illustrated book containing a representative of each of the approved breeds. Ch. Zepherine Lysander, a tricolor dog bred in England by Mrs. M. J. Birchall, was chosen by the editor and appeared on page 259. Owned by Jane Esther Henderson of Stockton, New Jersey, Lysander won 52 Bests of Variety, a Group One at New Brunswick and 4 other Group placements. His half sister Ch. Zepherine Collette, also by Lucian of Lavenderway, nearly equaled his record. Mrs. Henderson also purchased the American-bred Ch. Vica Red Ned CD among others for her collection.

During this period another tricolor, Ch. Smudge Face of Egypt, whose owner Joan Higgins stated he was only shown an average of 6 or 7 times a year, won the Variety at Eastern Dog Club for 4 shows in succession and at South Shore for 6 consecutive years, totaling 25 Bests of Variety. Bred at Godric kennels, formerly the "of Egypt" prefix, his sire and dam were both Irish imports.

Following these pioneers there were Brynmar, Doublejay, Luary, Richard Thomas's Fotheringay, Harvey Cookman's

Ch. Dreamridge Dear Hyatt, bred by Tom O'Neal, was an all-breed Best in Show dog and was the number-one English Toy Spaniel in the US in 1994.

Harco and Susan Jackson's Suruca. The 1970s ushered in Kingscourt, Ebonwood, Danaho, Pauline Patterson's Amerglo in California and Tom O'Neal's Dreamridge in Illinois. Sue Jackson of Indiana is still active, and her Ruby class dog, Southdown Notwithstanding, won the 2006 English Toy Spaniel Club of America (ETSCA) national specialty in May while Thomas Kilcullen of Ebonwood has the occasional litter in between his judging assignments.

Dana Hopkins of Danaho continues to successfully exhibit in California. Ch. Clancy of Double Jay, a tricolor dog bred by Juliana Bitters and co-owned with Elizabeth Crawford, made a significant appearance in the

1980s by winning a Best in Show and producing 13 champions, including 3 ranked in the top ten winners in the breed.

In the last decade or so Christina Van Patten's Royalist Blenheims and Prince Charles have established themselves by blending the Tudorhurst and Dreamridge lines and consistently winning Groups and earning Group placements, while the King Charles and Rubies of Sue Kisielewski in Virginia continue to earn their championships. Vanessa Weber's Kenjockety kennel, based in Connecticut, has imported numerous dogs in recent years, while Dr. Michael White and Richard LeBeau's Beauprix English Toys regularly appear in the top ratings. In Oregon the Cheri-A kennels of John Wood and Jerome Elliott exhibited a top winner in 1987 and 1988, Ch. Oakridges The Chimes, who went on to sire the Best in Show (BIS) Ch. Cheri-A Lord Andrew. In 2000 their bitch Ch. Cheri-A Lady Isabella Smokey Valley earned several Bests in Show and won the national specialty under Mr. Norman Patton in 2000. More recently, the Eli-Fran kennels of Frank and Karen Pouder have accounted for several homebred champions including the top winner for several years, Ch. Eli-Fran's Sir William.

The name Dreamridge comes to the forefront after 25 years of historic success. Ch. Dreamridge Daphne of Kings Court, a black and tan, was the first bitch to win an all-breed Best in Show and won the national specialty three years in a row from 1983 to 1985. Ch. Dreamridge Dear Charles won 20 Toy Groups and 3 Bests in Show while the Blenheim, Ch. Dreamridge Dear Jeffrey ROM, was also a Best in Show and national specialty winner. He went on to sire Ch. Dreamridge Dear Sir ROM, the national winner in 1990 and the sire of yet another BIS dog, Ch. Eli-Fran's Sir William. Ch. Dreamridge Dear Buzz was twice a Best in Show winner and also won the 1988 national. Ch. Dreamridge Dear Hyatt, owned by the late Chris Thaxton, was another Best in Show dog as well as the 1994 and 1995 Pedigree Award winner. The Dreamridge-owned dogs were always presented by Ron Fabis, who served as president of the ETSCA for many years and whose death left a vast and unfillable void.

A significant prefix that emerged during this period was Dr. Bob and Deb Bowman's Debonaire. Their original interest was in Cocker Spaniels, thus their close association with Tom O'Neal's Dreamridge, as he created records in that breed prior to his interest in the English Toys, both having won the American Spaniel Club's national futurities. Ch. Debonaire Double Jeopardy was a multiple Best in Show dog and a four-time national specialty winner. Two brothers from the repeat mating were Group winners and ranked in the top five nationally in the years that they were shown. Sadly, Dr. Bowman passed away unexpectedly in the late 1990s.

The English Toy Spaniel Club of America is the official parent club of the breed, and their membership numbers have remained steady for decades at approximately 60. In 2005 there was a small surge that boosted the total to over 70 members. The club's first national specialty show was held in 1981 in Illinois and was judged by the revered dog authority, Mrs. Anne Rogers Clark, who chose from an impressive entry the King Charles dog, Ch. Harco's Towncrier. This dog also has the distinction of being the first of his variety to place in the Toy Group at the Westminster Kennel Club, achieving a Group Four in 1979. This respected dog was nearing nine years of age at the time he captured the eye of Mrs. Clark and, even more remarkably, he was the sire of the dog that won both of the Toy Groups and Best in Show at the all-breed

Bred in England by Alicia Pennington and imported to America by Christina Van Patten, Ch. Tudorhurst Thespian ranked in the top ten English Toy Spaniels for two years.

to judge the King Charles entry at the all-breed exhibition the day before the inaugural event. She remarked on the good construction of the whole colors and praised the American breeders for their devotion.

While often there will be only one or two English Toys exhibited at a show, many have managed to rise to the top, defeating all of the other breeds despite lesser popularity and numbers. Currently a Prince Charles holds the Best in Show record for the breed with 11 wins, more than any other English Toy Spaniel in history. Ch. Loujon Backroad Adventure ("Venture") was bred in America by a noted English Springer Spaniel breeder, Karen Miller, whose attention has been captured by the "Charlies," as the breed is affectionately known. This dog is sired by a French import who also has achieved the pinnacle of success in dogdom, Best in Show. Recently Venture traveled to France, the birthplace of his sire, and defeated an impressive gathering of the breed, winning the French national specialty, judged by a well-known English authority, Bill Moffet.

The only independent English Toy Spaniel club in America other than the ETSCA was founded in 1995 by the late B.J. Miller of Walnut Creek,

shows that weekend, Ch. Dreamridge Dear Charles.

The ETSCA holds a national event every year in late May with breeders and exhibitors traveling from all over the country to participate with their best. There have been 9 King Charles, 2 Rubies, 14 Prince Charles and one Blenheim to achieve top honors at the annual national specialty. This original historic Illinois weekend was additionally noteworthy as Alicia Pennington of the renowned Tudorhurst kennels in Essex, England was persuaded

California. A lifetime dog fancier beginning with his mother's English Setters, B.J. became enamored of the English Toy, importing a Tudorhurst dog among others. Despite sharing his home with only a few beloved dogs, he owner-handled them to impressive wins, including the 1998 national specialty. B.J.'s efforts on behalf of the breed brought forth the Camino Real English Toy Spaniel Club, which held its inaugural specialty in 2000, drawing an entry of 80 and was won by Ch. Royalist Reign On.

The relatively recent advent of agility activities has opened up limitless possibilities for this intelligent and sturdy charmer. The year 2005 saw nine agility titles earned by Charlies.

This rare breed's unique little face makes unexpected appearances in unusual places. In 2001, when Mr. and Mrs. Burt Rapoport opened Henry's, a chic eatery in Delray Beach, Florida, they hung an 8-foot-high oil painting of Debbie's beloved Prince Charles in a prominent place. In the 1920s and 1930s, when cigarettes were the rage, Players and Wills offered collectible cards that were originally sealed in cigarette packs with illustrations of various dog breeds. The English Toy Spaniel was quite popular, and there were several different paintings used of the different colors, full body as well as head studies. These cards are still highly sought after.

In 1997 Royal Fireworks Press published a charming little children's book entitled *Blue Ribbons For Juliet* by Marilyn M. Lowery. The star is a champion tricolor female named Juliet, acquired from Dana Hopkins of Danaho kennels. Pauline Patterson of Amerglo and her daughter, Sheri Martinez, handled Juliet to her championship as well as eleven Bests of Breed. The story chronicles her adventures with a boy named Tristan. This is truly an international breed and a rare jewel.

Ch. Royalist Blaze of Glory (LEFT) was Best of Winners and Best Bred by Exhibitor in Show at the 2002 ETSCA national. Ch. Royalist American Beauty (RIGHT) was the top English Toy bitch all-systems in 2006.

Original watercolor paintings of English Toy Spaniels by Michael Allen.

CHARACTERISTICS OF THE
ENGLISH TOY SPANIEL

The English Toy Spaniel is a wonderful little dog! He is not only aristocratic but also cute and smart. Several of them can easily live with you in a small apartment as well as ride with you in the car. They are easy to carry on trains or subways, as they will fit in small baskets or carriers. Your English Toy can travel on an airplane in a small crate that will fit under your seat. In addition, they eat little compared to larger breeds and clean-up chores are also considerably easier! The English Toy is a quick learner and, in a short period of time, your little Charlie will turn into a charming gentleman or lady that will be a joy to live with.

Unlike the gundogs from which the English Toy derives, he is small and will not be a companion for a two-mile run or a ten-lap swim around the pool. He will not chase down rabbits, and he will not pick up fallen birds. However, if you like a small, sophisticated dog who is easy to live with, easy to maintain and will be your companion for life, then you are looking in the right place. Once you give your heart and home to an English Toy Spaniel, you will remain a devotee of the breed for life.

If you have young children in your household at the time that you purchase your puppy, you must be certain that they are aware that this is a small dog and that he will remain so for his lifetime. This is not a dog suited to rough-and-tumble play as would be a sporting dog like a Golden Retriever or an English Springer Spaniel. The English Toy weighs no more than 14 lbs as an adult, and he should be handled with care. He must not be dropped, sat upon or pushed around.

The English Toy has a steady disposition and fits in easily with family life. He gets along well with children and will accept strangers once he has had a chance to look them over. He can also be a good little indoor watchdog. The breed is

The Charlie's small size enables him to fit into any home. Add to that the breed's delightful personality and distinguished looks, and you may find it hard to stop at just one!

clean and quiet and has a soft and appealing expression. English Toys are elegant, cheerful, very affectionate and devoted companions. They are sweet and delicate due to size, but they are also sturdy. They have a selfless temperament and an ego-less disposition. What more could you want in a little companion?

THE DECISION TO BUY A PURE-BRED DOG

Certainly the Charlie's distinctive appearance and character have captured your fancy, and thus you are considering the purchase of a pure-bred dog. There are many predictable traits that recommend pure-bred dogs over mixed-breed dogs. It is almost impossible to determine what a mixed-breed puppy will look like as an adult. More importantly, it is impossible to determine what the temperament of a puppy of mixed parentage is going to be like. Will he be suitable for the person or family who wishes to own him? If the puppy grows up to be too big, too hairy or too active for the owner, what then will happen?

Size and temperament can vary to a degree, even within pure-bred dogs. Still, controlled breeding over many generations has produced dogs that give us reasonable assurance of what a pure-bred puppy will look and act like when he reaches maturity. This predictability is more important than you might think.

Just about any dog whose background is made up of sound individuals has the potential to be a loving companion. However, the predictability of a pure-bred dog offers reasonable insurance that the dog will suit not only the owner's esthetic demands but also that person's lifestyle. Before you bring an English Toy Spaniel puppy into your household, visit breeders and spend as much time with both puppies and adults as you can. You must confirm that the adult English Toy Spaniel is the dog that appeals to you esthetically and temperamentally, and above all, be certain that you will in fact be a suitable owner for the breed.

HEART-HEALTHY

In this modern age of ever-improving cardio-care, no doctor or scientist can dispute the advantages of owning a dog to lower a person's risk of heart disease. Studies have proven that petting a dog, walking a dog and grooming a dog all show positive results toward lowering your blood pressure. The simple routine of exercising your dog—going outside with the dog and walking, jogging or playing catch—is heart-healthy in and of itself. If you are normally less active than your physician thinks you should be, adopting a dog may be a smart option to improve your own quality of life as well as that of another creature.

HEALTH CONSIDERATIONS FOR THE ENGLISH TOY SPANIEL

All pure-bred dogs are predisposed to some hereditary health concerns, and the English Toy is no exception. As a prospective owner of this breed, you should be aware of these potential problems and understand what they are about. By buying your puppy from a reputable breeder who is knowledgeable about these problems, you are making the most responsible first step possible. Openly discuss all of the following with your chosen breeder and ask to see health-testing documentation such as patellar and cardiac clearances from the Orthopedic Foundation for Animals (OFA) and eye clearances from the Canine Eye Registration Foundation (CERF).

If you're always on the go, your English Toy Spaniel can join you! Easy portability is yet another plus with this compact toy dog.

LUXATED KNEECAPS OR PATELLAR LUXATION

Common to most small breeds, this is an important problem and it has been reported for well over 100 years in the English Toy. Due to careful breeding, as this is usually an inherited fault, it is not as prominent as it was at one time although it still is considered the biggest health issue in the breed. The patella, or kneecap, deviates to the inside of the leg so that the muscles of the leg responsible for straightening the knee are no longer in alignment. The result can range from little or no lameness to complete non-use of the leg.

Your veterinarian should be contacted if you suspect that your dog has this problem. The vet will manipulate the stifle joint to see if he can push the kneecap in or out of position. Your vet should determine if your dog is a candidate for surgery.

HEART DISEASE

Patent ductus arteriosis (PDA) is one of the more common congenital cardiac problems in dogs of all breeds and is sometimes reported in the English Toy. This condition occurs when the blood vessel connecting the fetus's aorta and pulmonary artery does not close within a week or so after the puppy's birth. When the blood

An example of the Blenheim variety of the English Toy Spaniel.

vessel remains open, it causes a "leak," resulting in extra work for the puppy's left ventricle.

Conventional treatment is to surgically close the opening. The prognosis is good for most affected dogs when PDA is caught early and treated. Diagnosis is usually made through detection of a heart murmur during a pup's routine veterinary exam and then confirmed by further testing. However, symptoms that the owner may recognize include breathing difficulties and/or coughing, lethargy/collapse during exercise and a bluish cast to the mucous membranes. Any of these symptoms warrant veterinary attention.

Another heart problem, imitral valve disease, is a prevalent problem in the Cavalier King Charles Spaniel and also has been seen in the English Toy.

EYE DISEASE

Some eye problems that are common to many breeds have been seen in the English Toy. These include glaucoma, cataract and retinal dysplasia. A dog can be predisposed to glaucoma and/or cataracts genetically, but both conditions also can occur as a result of trauma to the eye. Retinal dysplasia is most often hereditary; in the English Toy this occurs mostly in the form of retinal folds, which cause small areas of blindness which may not significantly affect a dog's vision.

DIABETES MELLITUS

This can affect middle-aged to older bitches. Early signs of diabetes are frequent urination, excessive drinking of water, a large appetite or unexplained weight loss. With early diagnosis and proper care, life for the dog can be prolonged.

BREATHING DIFFICULTIES

The English Toy Spaniel has a pushed-in nose like the Pekingese or Japanese Chin. These breeds have abnormally small openings to the nostrils and relatively long palates. Dogs prefer to breathe through their noses and, for these breeds, it becomes difficult to breathe through the small nasal openings. Thus the dog must increase his respiratory effort even when at rest.

Because of their breathing problems, English Toy Spaniels can be very susceptible to heat

and cold; caution must be taken, particularly in the summer months. Your dog must never be given strenuous activity in the heat, and he must not be out in the cold any longer than necessary. Abnormal noises, such as snorting and snoring, are also common with these breeds.

Although this list of health problems may look daunting, English Toy Spaniels are still considered to be a healthy breed. The problems mentioned are possible in the breed and a buyer should be aware of them. Some of these diseases are rare and most of them only turn up on occasion. Do not be turned away from the breed but do be aware that if the breeder of your puppy is reputable, and thus aware of these problems, he will be doing his best to breed them out of his line, never using a carrier of an hereditary disease as a breeding animal.

COMMON IN THE BREED...

The following are commonly seen in the ETS and, under typical circumstances, are not considered health problems:

- Open fontanelle: A soft spot on the top of the skull that does not close right away as the pup grows. You should make your vet aware of this, but it should not be an issue in dogs under one year of age.
- Umbilical hernia: A small bit of the intestine or tissue that protrudes through the umbilical cord ring and fails to close. This may heal on its own or leave a small "bubble" of tissue; only in the case of a larger hernia that remains open is surgery necessary. If surgery is required, it is recommended to have it performed while the dog is anesthetized for another reason, such as spaying or neutering, to reduce the amount of times that he must be under anesthesia.
- Fused toes: Not all English Toys have fused toes, but they are fairly common in the breed and even mentioned as acceptable in the breed standard.

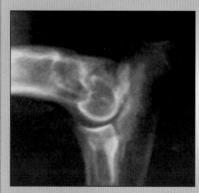

An x-ray showing a dogs' knee joint, including his kneecap (patellas). Patellar luxation has been an inherited problem in the breed for more than a century, but careful breeding continues to lessen its incidence.

ENGLISH TOY SPANIEL

The breed standard is a written description of what is believed to be the perfect specimen of a breed. A standard is required for every pure-bred breed of dog. The standard gives breeders and judges a mental image of what the ideal representative of the breed should look like. Reputable breeders, therefore, strive to produce animals that will meet the qualifications depicted in the standard. Judges use the standard to determine how closely the dogs presented in the show ring conform to the ideal. The dog that most closely conforms to the standard, in the judge's opinion, is the Best of Breed for the day. This is the concept that governs conformation shows.

A well-bred English Toy Spaniel should look like a proper spaniel and he will have the personality, disposition and intelligence that are sought after in the breed. The standard details the breed's physical attributes (head, mouth, neck, color, coat, etc.) as well as the breed's temperament, characteristics and movement or gait.

Standards originally were written by fanciers who had a love and a concern for the breed. These early dog fanciers, many of whom were horse people who knew mammal anatomy and took much of the terminology for granted, understood the basics of proper construction. These people also recognized that the essential characteristics of the English Toy Spaniel were unlike those of any other breed and that care (through a written breeding and judging standard) must be taken that these characteristics were maintained through the generations.

As time progressed, new generations of dog folk needed more details to better understand canine construction. Most of the new blood were not horse people. Thus breeders became more aware that certain areas of the dog needed a better description, and they would get together and work out a revised, more detailed standard. Breed standards change very little over the years and are never revised on a whim. Serious study and exchange between experts and breeders take place before any move is made. In the US, the recognized national parent club formulates the standard for the breed and submits it to the AKC for acceptance.

THE AMERICAN KENNEL CLUB STANDARD FOR THE ENGLISH TOY SPANIEL

General Appearance: The English Toy Spaniel is a compact, cobby and essentially square toy dog possessed of a short-nosed, domed head, a merry and affectionate demeanor and a silky, flowing coat. His compact, sturdy body and charming temperament, together with his rounded head, lustrous dark eye and well cushioned face, proclaim him a dog of distinction and character. The important characteristics of the breed are exemplified by the head.

Size, Proportion, Substance: *Size*—The most desirable weight of an adult is 8 to 14 pounds. General symmetry and substance

Just as judges use the breed standard to evaluate dogs in the ring, breeders use it to determine the quality of young maturing dogs.

A study in color, with each variety represented: Ruby, King Charles, Blenheim and Prince Charles.

are more important than the actual weight; however, all other things being equal, the smaller sized dog is to be preferred. *Proportion*—Compact and essentially square in shape, built on cobby lines. *Substance*—Sturdy of frame, solidly constructed.

Head: Head large in comparison to size, with a plush, chubby look, albeit with a degree of refinement which prevents it from being coarse.

Expression: Soft and appealing, indicating an intelligent nature.

Eyes: Large and very dark brown or black, set squarely on line with the nose, with little or no white showing. The eye rims should be black.

Ears: Very long and set low and close to the head, fringed with heavy feathering.

Skull: High and well domed; from the side, curves as far out over the eyes as possible.

Stop: Deep and well-defined.

Muzzle: Very short, with the nose well laid back and with well developed cushioning under the eyes.

Jaw: Square, broad and deep, and well turned up, with lips properly meeting to give a finished appearance.

Nose: Large and jet black in color, with large, wide open nostrils.

Bite: Slightly undershot; teeth not to show. A wry mouth should be penalized; a hanging tongue is extremely objectionable.

Neck, Topline, Body: *Neck*— Moderate in length; nicely arched. *Topline*—Level. *Body*— Short, compact, square and deep, on cobby lines, with a broad back. Sturdy of frame, with good rib and deep brisket.

Tail: The tail is docked to 2 to 4 inches in length and carried at or just slightly above the level of the back. The set of the tail is at the back's level. Many are born with a shorter or screw tail which is acceptable. The feather on the tail should be silky and from 3 to 4 inches in length, constituting a marked "flag" of a square shape. The tail and its carriage is an index of the breed's attitude and character.

A mature dog with a luxurious coat. He exhibits proper balance and proportion. He is structurally sound and typey. His tail is docked and fully tasseled.

Head study of a mature dog showing pleasing type, expression, structure, balance and proportion.

the chest, and with flowing feathering on both the front and hind legs, and feathering on the feet. The coat is straight or only slightly wavy, with a silken, glossy texture. Although the Blenheim and the Ruby rarely gain the length of coat and ears of the Prince Charles and King Charles, good coats and long ear fringes are a desired and prized attribute. Over-trimming of the body, feet or tail fringings should be penalized.

Color: The Blenheim (red and white) consists of a pearly white ground with deep red or chestnut markings evenly distributed in large patches. The ears and the cheeks are red, with a blaze of white extending from the nose up the forehead and ending between the ears in a crescentic curve. It is preferable that there be red markings around both eyes. The Blenheim often carries a thumb mark or "Blenheim Spot" placed on the top and the center of the skull.

The Prince Charles (tricolor) consists of a pearly white ground, with evenly distributed black patches, solid black ears and black face markings. It is prefer-able that there be black markings

Forequarters: Shoulders well laid back; legs well boned and strong, dropping straight down from the elbow; strong in pastern. Feet, front and rear, are neat and compact; fused toes are often seen and are acceptable.

Hindquarters: Rear legs are well muscled and nicely angulated to indicate strength, and parallel of hock.

Coat: Profusely coated, heavy fringing on the ears, body and on around both eyes. The tan markings are of a rich color, and on the face, over the eyes, in the lining of the ears, and under the tail.

The King Charles (black and tan) is a rich, glossy black with bright mahogany tan markings appearing on the cheeks, lining of the ears, over the eyes, on the legs and underneath the tail. The presence of a small white chest patch about the size of a quarter, or a few white hairs on the chest of a King Charles Spaniel are not to be penalized; other white markings are an extremely serious fault.

The Ruby is a self-colored, rich mahogany red. The presence of a small white chest patch about the size of a quarter, or a few white hairs on the chest of a Ruby Spaniel are not to be penalized. Other white markings are an extremely serious fault.

Gait: Elegant with good reach in the front, and sound, driving rear action. The gait as a whole is free and lively, evidencing stable character and correct construction. In profile, the movement exhibits a good length of stride, and viewed from front and rear it is straight and true, resulting from straight-boned fronts and properly made and muscled hindquarters.

Temperament: The English Toy Spaniel is a bright and interested

FAULTS IN PROFILE

Both of these dogs have nice heads, but there it ends. This dog is long-bodied and low on leg. He is roach-backed and lacks angulation at both ends. He is narrow in front and toes out. He has no neck.

This dog is wide in front with weak pasterns and flat feet. He has a dip behind his upright shoulders and is high in the rear. He is weak behind and cowhocked. He has a bit too much leg beneath him.

little dog, affectionate and willing to please.

Approved June 13, 1989
Effective August 1, 1989

A regal breed with a noble past, the English Toy Spaniel is an attractive and charming companion.

ENGLISH TOY SPANIEL

WHERE TO BEGIN

If you are convinced that the English Toy Spaniel is the ideal dog for you, it's time to learn about where to find a puppy and what to look for. Locating a litter of English Toy Spaniels will take some patience as the breed is relatively rare. You should inquire about breeders in your region of the country who enjoy a good reputation in the breed. Although the breed is not numerically strong in most countries, it is possible to locate dedicated breeders with a bit of research. Fortunately, the majority of English Toy Spaniel breeders are devoted to the breed and its well-being. The parent club for the breed, the English Toy Spaniel Club of America, is a trusted source for breeder referrals and can be contacted online at www.etsca.org. Club members can direct you to a reputable breeder who doesn't live on the other side of the country.

Potential owners are encouraged to attend dog shows to see the English Toy Spaniels in person, to meet the owners and handlers firsthand and to get an idea of what English Toy Spaniels look like outside a photographer's lens. Provided you approach the handlers when they are not busy with the dogs, most are more than willing to answer questions,

SIGNS OF A HEALTHY PUPPY

Healthy puppies are robust little fellows who are alert and active, sporting shiny coats and supple skin. They should not appear lethargic, bloated or pot-bellied nor should they have flaky skin or runny or crusted eyes or noses. Their stool should be firm and well formed, with no evidence of blood or mucus.

A SHOW PUPPY

If you plan to show your puppy, you must first deal with a reputable breeder who shows his dogs and has had some success in the conformation ring. The puppy's pedigree should include one or more champions in the first and second generation. You should be familiar with the breed and breed standard so you can know what qualities to look for in your puppy. The breeder's observations and recommendations also are invaluable aids in selecting your future champion. If you consider an older puppy, be sure that the puppy has been properly socialized with people and not isolated in a kennel without substantial daily human contact.

recommend breeders and give advice.

Once you have contacted and met a breeder or two and made your choice about which breeder is best suited to your needs, it's time to visit the litter when one becomes available. Since you are likely to be choosing an English Toy Spaniel as a pet dog and not a show dog, you simply should select a pup that is friendly, attractive and healthy. Charlies generally have small litters, averaging four puppies, so selection is limited once you have located a desirable litter.

Unlike most breeds of dog, the English Toy has an undershot bite, and this will be evident in a young puppy. The color of the puppy is another consideration, as there are four attractive varieties in the breed: solid red, black and tan, tricolored and deep red or chestnut and white. Each variety has its own appeal. Discuss colors with the breeder. Some varieties may be easier to acquire in certain regions, while others may require a bit more patience until an available puppy arrives. There is no difference in character or health between the varieties.

Breeders commonly allow visitors to see their litters by around the fifth or sixth week, and puppies leave for their new homes around the ninth or tenth week. English Toy puppies are especially fragile and should not be released any earlier. Breeders who permit their puppies to leave early are more interested in your dollars than in their puppies' well-being. Puppies need to learn the rules of the pack from their dams, and most dams continue teaching the pups manners and dos and don'ts until they leave for new homes. Breeders spend significant amounts of time with the English Toy Spaniel toddlers so that the pups are able to interact with the "other species," i.e., humans. Given the long history that dogs and humans have, bonding between the two species is natural but must be nurtured. A well-bred, well-socialized English Toy Spaniel pup wants nothing more than to be near you and please you.

A COMMITTED NEW OWNER

By now you should understand what makes the English Toy Spaniel a most unique and special dog, one that may fit nicely into your family and lifestyle. If you have researched breeders, you should be able to recognize a knowledgeable and responsible English Toy Spaniel breeder who cares not only about his pups but also about what kind of owner you will be. If you have completed the next step in your new journey, you have found a litter, or possibly two, of quality English Toy Spaniel pups.

A visit with the puppies and

CREATE A SCHEDULE

Puppies thrive on sameness and routine. Offer meals at the same time each day, take him out at regular times for potty trips and do the same for play periods and outdoor activity. Make note of when your puppy naps and when he is most lively and energetic, and try to plan his day around those times. Once he is house-trained and more predictable in his habits, he will be better able to tolerate changes in his schedule.

their breeder should be an education in itself. Breed research, breeder selection and puppy visitation are very important aspects of finding the puppy of your dreams. Beyond that, these things also lay the foundation for a successful future with your pup. Puppy personalities within each litter vary, from the shy and easy-

A look at the pups' quarters tells volumes about the care they are receiving from the breeder. Good care also is evident in clear eyes, shiny coats, alert temperaments and the overall impression of health.

going puppy to the one who is dominant and assertive, with most pups falling somewhere in between. By spending time with the puppies you will be able to recognize certain behaviors and what these behaviors indicate about each pup's temperament. Which type of pup will complement your family dynamics is best determined by observing the puppies in action within their "pack." Your breeder's expertise and recommendations are so valuable. Although you may fall in love with a bold and brassy male, the breeder may suggest that another pup would be best for you. The breeder's experience in rearing English Toy Spaniel pups and matching their temperaments with appropriate humans offers the best assurance that your pup will meet your needs and expectations. The type of puppy that you select is just as important as your decision that the English Toy Spaniel is the breed for you.

The decision to live with a Charlie is a serious commitment and not one to be taken lightly. This puppy is a living sentient being that will be dependent on you for basic survival for his entire life. Beyond the basics of survival—food, water, shelter and protection—he needs much, much more. The new pup needs love, nurturing and a proper canine education to mold him into a responsible, well-behaved canine citizen. Your English Toy Spaniel's health and good manners will need consistent monitoring and regular "tune-ups," so your job as a responsible dog owner will be ongoing throughout every stage of his life. If you are not prepared to accept these responsibilities and commit to them for the dog's entire lifetime, then you are not prepared to own a dog of any breed.

MALE OR FEMALE?

Males of most dog breeds tend to be larger than their female counterparts and take longer to mature. Males also can be more dominant and territorial, especially if they are intact.
Neutering before one year of age can help minimize those tendencies.
Females of most breeds are often less rambunctious and easier to handle.
However, individual personalities vary, so the differences are often due more to temperament than to the sex of the animal.

NEW RELEASES

Breeders rarely release puppies until they are eight to ten weeks of age. This is an acceptable age for most breeds of dog, although toy-dog breeders may hold onto pups a little longer. English Toy pups go to new homes around nine weeks or older. If a breeder has a puppy that is 12 weeks of age or older, he is likely well socialized and house-trained.

Although the responsibilities of owning a dog may at times tax your patience, the joy of living with your English Toy Spaniel far outweighs the workload, and a well-mannered adult dog is worth your time and effort. Before your very eyes, your new charge will grow up to be your most loyal friend, devoted to you unconditionally.

YOUR ENGLISH TOY SPANIEL SHOPPING LIST

Just as expectant parents prepare a nursery for their baby, so should you ready your home for the arrival of your English Toy Spaniel pup. If you have the necessary puppy supplies purchased and in place before he comes home, it will ease the puppy's transition from the warmth and familiarity of his mom and littermates to the brand-new environment of his new home and human family. You will be too busy to stock up and prepare your house after your pup comes home, that's for sure. Imagine how a pup must feel upon being transported to a strange new place. It's up to you to comfort him and to let your little pup know that he is going to be happy with you.

FOOD AND WATER BOWLS
Your puppy will need separate bowls for his food and water. Stainless steel pans are generally preferred over plastic bowls since they sterilize better and pups are less inclined to chew on the metal. Heavy-duty ceramic bowls are popular, too, and many come in cute styles for your adorable English Toy. Buy adult-sized pans, as your puppy will grow into them before you know it.

Not all colors are available from every breeder, but, with such a selection, how will you choose?

The three most
popular crate
types: mesh on
the left, wire on
the right and
fiberglass on top.

The three most popular crate types: mesh on the left, wire on the right and fiberglass on top.

THE DOG CRATE

If you think that crates are tools of punishment and confinement for when a dog has misbehaved, think again. Most breeders and almost all trainers recommend a crate as the preferred house-training aid as well as for all-around puppy training and safety. Because dogs are natural den creatures that prefer cave-like environments, the benefits of crate use are many. The crate provides the puppy with his very own "safe house," a cozy place to sleep, take a break or seek comfort with a favorite toy; a travel aid to house your dog when on the road, at motels or at the vet's office; a training aid to help teach your puppy proper toileting habits; and a place of solitude when non-dog people happen to drop by and don't want a lively puppy—or even a well-behaved adult dog—saying hello or begging for attention.

Crates come in several types, although the wire crate and the fiberglass airline-type crate are the most popular. Both are safe and your puppy will adjust to either one, so the choice is up to you. The wire crates offer better visibility for the pup as well as better ventilation. Many of the wire crates easily fold into suitcase-size carriers. The fiberglass crates, similar to those used by the airlines for animal transport, are sturdier and more den-like. However, the fiberglass crates do not fold down and are less ventilated than a wire crate, and so can be problematic in hot weather. Some of the newer crates are made of heavy plastic mesh; they

CRATE EXPECTATIONS

To make the crate more inviting to your puppy, you can offer his first meal or two inside the crate, always keeping the crate door open so that he does not feel confined. Keep a favorite toy or two in the crate for him to play with while inside. You can also cover the crate at night with a lightweight sheet to make it more den-like and remove the stimuli of household activity. Never put him into his crate as punishment or as you are scolding him, since he will then associate his crate with negative situations and avoid going there.

MAKE A COMMITMENT

Dogs are most assuredly man's best friend, but they are also a lot of work. When you add a puppy to your family, you also are adding to your daily responsibilities for years to come. Dogs need more than just food, water and a place to sleep. They also require training (which can be ongoing throughout the lifetime of the dog), activity to keep them physically and mentally fit and hands-on attention every day, plus grooming and healthcare. Your life as you now know it may well disappear! Are you prepared for such drastic changes?

are very lightweight and fold up into slim-line suitcases. However, a mesh crate might not be suitable for a pup with manic chewing habits.

Purchase a small crate for your Charlie, which should give him room to stand up and lie down comfortably and will suit him both as a puppy and when fully grown.

BEDDING AND CRATE PADS

Your puppy will enjoy some type of soft bedding in his "room" (the crate), something he can snuggle into to feel cozy and secure. Old towels or blankets are good choices for a young pup, since he may (and probably will) have a toileting accident or two in the crate or decide to chew on the

bedding material. Once he is fully trained and out of the early chewing stage, you can replace the puppy bedding with a permanent crate pad if you prefer. Crate pads and other dog beds run the gamut from inexpensive to high-end doggie-designer styles, but don't splurge on the good stuff until you are sure that your puppy is reliable and won't tear it up or make a mess on it.

PUPPY TOYS

Just as infants and older children require objects to stimulate their minds and bodies, puppies need toys to entertain their curious brains, wiggly paws and achy

Some crates easily can fit a small pack of English Toys, but crate training only works if each dog has his own personal crate, a "den" of his own.

TOYS 'R SAFE

The vast array of tantalizing puppy toys is staggering. Stroll through any pet shop or pet-supply outlet and you will see that the choices can be overwhelming. However, not all dog toys are safe or sensible. Most very young puppies enjoy soft woolly toys that they can snuggle with and carry around. (You know they have outgrown them when they shred them up!) Avoid toys that have buttons, tabs or other enhancements that can be chewed off and swallowed. Soft toys that squeak are fun, but make sure your puppy does not disembowel the toy and remove (and swallow) the squeaker. Toys that rattle or make noise can excite a puppy, but they present the same danger as the squeaky kind and so require supervision. Hard rubber toys that bounce can also entertain a pup, but make sure that the toy is too big for your pup to swallow.

teeth. A fun array of safe doggie toys will help satisfy your puppy's chewing instincts and distract him from gnawing on the leg of your antique chair or your new leather sofa. Most puppy toys are cute and look as if they would be a lot of fun, but not all are necessarily safe or good for your puppy, so use caution when you go puppy-toy shopping.

English Toy Spaniel puppies like soft toys and generally are not very energetic chewers, so should not be too problematic in this regard. Squeaky toys are quite popular and should only be offered under careful supervision. The best "chewcifiers" are nylon and hard rubber bones, which are safe to gnaw on and come in sizes appropriate for all age groups and breeds. Be especially careful of natural bones, which can splinter or develop dangerous sharp edges; dogs can easily swallow or choke on those bone splinters. Veterinarians often tell of surgical nightmares involving bits of splintered bone, because in addition to the danger of choking, the sharp pieces can damage the intestinal tract.

Similarly, rawhide chews, while a favorite of most dogs and puppies, can be equally dangerous. Pieces of rawhide are easily swallowed after they get soft and gummy from chewing, and dogs have been known to choke on pieces of ingested rawhide.

Rawhide chews should be offered only when you can supervise the puppy.

Soft woolly toys are special puppy favorites. They come in a wide variety of cute shapes and sizes; some look like little stuffed animals. Puppies love to shake them up and toss them about or simply carry them around. Be careful of fuzzy toys that have button eyes or noses that your pup could chew off and swallow, and make sure that he does not disembowel a squeaky toy to remove the squeaker! Braided rope toys are similar in that they are fun to chew and toss around, but they shred easily and the strings are easy to swallow. The strings are not digestible and, if the puppy doesn't pass them in his stool, he could end up at the vet's office. As with rawhides, your puppy should be closely monitored with rope toys.

If you believe that your pup has ingested a piece of one of his toys, check his stools for the next couple of days to see if he passes the item when he defecates. At the same time, also watch for signs of intestinal distress. A call to your veterinarian might be in order to get his advice and be on the safe side.

An all-time favorite toy for puppies (young and old!) is the empty gallon milk jug. Hard plastic juice containers—46 ounces or more—are also excellent. Such containers make lots of noise when they are batted about, and puppies go crazy with delight as they play with them. However, they don't often last very long, so be sure to remove and replace them when they get chewed up.

A word of caution about homemade toys: be careful with your choices of non-traditional play objects. Never use old shoes

SELECTING FROM THE LITTER
Before you visit a litter of puppies, promise yourself that you won't fall for the first pretty face you see! Decide on your goals for your puppy—show prospect, obedience competitor, family companion—and then look for a puppy who displays the appropriate qualities. In most litters, there is an alpha pup (the bossy puppy), and occasionally a shy fellow who is less confident, with the rest of the litter falling somewhere in the middle. "Middle-of-the-roaders" are safe bets for most families and novice competitors.

Check the collar often, as puppies grow in spurts, and his collar can become too tight almost overnight. Choke collars should never be used on small dogs like the English Toy Spaniel.

LEASHES

A 6-foot nylon lead is an excellent choice for a young puppy. It is lightweight and not as tempting to chew as a leather lead. You can switch to a 6-foot leather lead after your pup has grown and is used to walking politely on a lead. For initial puppy walks and house-training purposes, you should invest in a shorter lead so that you have more control over the puppy. At first, you don't want him wandering too far away from you, and when taking him out for toileting you will want to keep him in the specific area chosen for his potty spot.

The quick-click collar is one of the most popular and versatile collars on the market and comes in a variety of designs.

or socks, since a puppy cannot distinguish between the old ones on which he's allowed to chew and the new ones in your closet that are strictly off limits. That principle applies to anything that resembles something that you don't want your puppy to chew.

COLLARS

A lightweight nylon collar is the best choice for a very young pup. Quick-click collars are easy to put on and remove, and they can be adjusted as the puppy grows. Introduce him to his collar as soon as he comes home to get him accustomed to wearing it. He'll get used to it quickly and won't mind a bit. Make sure that it is snug enough that it won't slip off yet loose enough to be comfortable for the pup. You should be able to slip two fingers between the collar and his neck.

GETTING ACQUAINTED

When visiting a litter, ask the breeder for suggestions on how best to interact with the puppies. If possible, get right into the middle of the pack and sit down with them. Observe which pups climb into your lap and which ones shy away. Toss a toy for them to chase and bring back to you. It's easy to fall in love with the first puppy who picks you, but keep your future objectives in mind before you make your final decision.

Once the puppy is heel-trained with a traditional leash, you can consider purchasing a retractable lead. A retractable lead is excellent for walking adult dogs that are already leash-wise. This type of lead allows the dog to roam farther away from you and explore a wider area when out walking, and also retracts when you need to keep him close to you.

HOME SAFETY FOR YOUR PUPPY

The importance of puppy-proofing cannot be overstated. In addition to making your house comfortable for your English Toy Spaniel's arrival, you also must make sure that your house is safe for your puppy before you bring him home. There are countless hazards in the owner's personal living environment that a pup can sniff, chew, swallow or destroy. Many are obvious; others are not. Do a thorough advance house check to remove or rearrange those things that could hurt your puppy, keeping any potentially dangerous items out of areas to which he will have access.

Electrical cords are especially dangerous, since puppies view them as irresistible chew toys. Unplug and remove all exposed cords or fasten them beneath baseboards where the puppy cannot reach them. Veterinarians and firefighters can tell you horror stories

TEETHING TIME

All puppies chew. It's normal canine behavior. Chewing just plain feels good to a puppy, especially during the three- to five-month teething period when the adult teeth are breaking through the gums. Rather than attempting to eliminate such a strong natural chewing instinct, you will be more successful if you redirect it and teach your puppy what he may or may not chew. Correct inappropriate chewing with a sharp "No!" and offer him a chew toy, praising him when he takes it. Don't become discouraged. Chewing usually decreases after the adult teeth have come in.

about electrical burns and house fires that resulted from puppy-chewed electrical cords. Consider this a most serious precaution for your puppy and the rest of your family.

Scout your home for tiny objects that might be seen at a

pup's eye level. Keep medication bottles and cleaning supplies well out of reach, and do the same with waste baskets and other trash containers. It goes without saying that you should not use rodent poison or other toxic chemicals in any puppy area and that you must keep such containers safely locked up. You will be amazed at how many places a curious puppy can discover!

Once your house has cleared inspection, check your yard. A sturdy fence, well embedded into the ground, will give your dog a safe place to play and potty. Fortunately, Charlies are not much interested in digging and should not try to "escape" in this

manner. Although English Toy Spaniels are not known to be climbers or fence jumpers either, they are still athletic dogs, so a 5- to 6-foot-high fence should be adequate to contain an agile youngster or adult. Check the fence periodically for necessary repairs. If there is a weak link or space to squeeze through, you can be sure a determined English Toy Spaniel will discover it.

The garage and shed can be hazardous places for a pup, as things like fertilizers, chemicals and tools are usually kept there. It's best to keep these areas off limits to the pup. Antifreeze is especially dangerous to dogs, as they find the taste appealing and it takes only a few licks from the driveway to kill a dog, puppy or adult, small breed or large.

VISITING THE VETERINARIAN

A good veterinarian is your English Toy Spaniel puppy's best health-insurance policy. If you do not already have a vet, ask friends and experienced dog people in your area for recommendations so that you can select a vet before you bring your English Toy Spaniel puppy home. Also arrange for your puppy's first veterinary examination before-hand, since many vets do not have appointments immediately available and your puppy should visit the vet within a day or so of coming home.

It's important to make sure your puppy's first visit to the vet is a pleasant and positive one. The vet should take great care to befriend the pup and handle him gently to make their first meeting a positive experience. The vet will give the pup a thorough physical examination and set up a sched-ule for vaccinations and other necessary wellness visits. Be sure to show your vet any health and inoculation records, which you should have received from your breeder. Your vet is a great source of canine health information, so be sure to ask questions and take notes. Creating a health journal for your puppy will make a handy reference for his wellness and any future health problems that may arise.

MEETING THE FAMILY

Your English Toy Spaniel's homecoming is an exciting time for all members of the family, and it's only natural that everyone will be eager to meet him, pet him and play with him. However, for the puppy's sake, it's best to make these initial family meetings as uneventful as possible so that the pup is not overwhelmed with too much too soon. Remember, he has just left his dam and his littermates and is away from the breeder's home for the first time. Despite his fuzzy wagging tail, he is still apprehensive and wondering where he is and who all these strange humans are. It's

---

KEEP OUT OF REACH

Most dogs don't browse around your medicine cabinet, but accidents do happen! The drug acetaminophen, the active ingredient in some over-the-counter pain relievers, can be deadly to dogs and cats if ingested in large quantities. Acetaminophen toxicity, caused by the dog's swallowing 15 to 20 tablets, can be manifested in abdominal pains within a day or two of ingestion, as well as liver damage. If you suspect your dog has swiped a bottle of medicine, get the dog to the vet immediately so that the vet can induce vomiting and cleanse the dog's stomach.

A Dog-Safe Home

The dog-safety police are taking you on a house tour. Let's go room by room and see how safe your own home is for your new English Toy Spaniel. The following items are doggy dangers, so either they must be removed or the dog should be monitored or not have access to these areas.

Outdoor
- swimming pool
- pesticides
- toxic plants
- lawn fertilizers

Living Room
- house plants (some varieties are poisonous)
- fireplace or wood-burning stove
- paint on the walls (lead-based paint is toxic)
- lead drapery weights (toxic lead)
- lamps and electrical cords
- carpet cleaners or deodorizers

Bathroom
- blue water in the toilet bowl
- medicine cabinet (filled with potentially deadly bottles)
- soap bars, bleach, drain cleaners, etc.
- tampons

Kitchen
- household cleaners in the kitchen cabinets
- glass jars and canisters
- sharp objects (like kitchen knives, scissors and forks)
- garbage can (with remnants of good-smelling things like onions, potato skins, apple or pear cores, peach pits, coffee beans, etc.)
- "people foods" that are toxic to dogs, like chocolate, raisins, grapes, nuts and onions

Garage
- antifreeze
- fertilizers (including rose foods)
- pesticides and rodenticides
- pool supplies (chlorine and other chemicals)
- oil and gasoline in containers
- sharp objects, electrical cords and power tools

best to let him explore on his own and meet the family members as he feels comfortable. Let him investigate all the new smells, sights and sounds at his own pace. Children should be especially careful to not get overly excited, use loud voices or hug the pup too tightly. Be calm, gentle and affectionate, and be ready to comfort him if he appears frightened or uneasy.

Be sure to show your puppy his new crate during this first day home. Toss a treat or two inside the crate; if he associates the crate with food, he will associate the crate with good things. If he is comfortable with the crate, you can offer him his first meal inside it. Leave the door ajar so he can wander in and out as he chooses.

FIRST NIGHT IN HIS NEW HOME

So much has happened in your English Toy Spaniel puppy's first day away from the breeder. He's had his first car ride to his new home. He's met his new human

family and perhaps the other family pets. He has explored his new house and yard, at least those places where he is to be allowed during his first weeks at home. He may have visited his new veterinarian. He has eaten his first meal or two away from his dam and littermates. Surely that's enough to tire out your young English Toy Spaniel pup—or so you hope!

It's bedtime. During the day, the pup investigated his crate, which is his new den and sleeping space, so it is not entirely strange to him. Line the crate with a soft towel or blanket that he can snuggle into and gently place him into the crate for the night. Some breeders send home a piece of bedding from where the pup slept with his littermates, and those familiar scents are a great comfort for the puppy on his first night without his siblings.

He will probably whine or cry. The puppy is objecting to the confinement and the fact that he

Charlies and dog toys go together. Get a good variety of safe toys for your pup.

THE FIRST FAMILY MEETING

Your puppy's first day at home should be quiet and uneventful. Despite his wagging tail, he is still wondering where his mom and siblings are! Let him make friends with other members of the family on his own terms; don't overwhelm him. You have a lifetime ahead to get to know each other!

is alone for the first time. This can be a stressful time for you as well as for the pup. It's important that you remain strong and don't let the puppy out of his crate to comfort him. He will fall asleep eventually. If you release him, the puppy will learn that crying means "out" and will continue that habit. You are laying the groundwork for future habits. Some breeders find that soft music

A close and lasting bond is the goal of proper early socialization with children.

can soothe a crying pup and help him get to sleep.

SOCIALIZING YOUR PUPPY
The first 20 weeks of your English Toy Spaniel puppy's life are the most important of his entire lifetime. A properly socialized puppy will grow up to be a confident and stable adult who will be a pleasure to live with and a welcome addition to the neighborhood.

The importance of socialization cannot be overemphasized. Research on canine behavior has proven that puppies who are not exposed to new sights, sounds, people and animals during their first 20 weeks of life will grow up to be timid and fearful, even aggressive, and unable to flourish outside of their familiar home environment.

Socializing your puppy is not difficult and, in fact, will be a fun time for you both. Lead training goes hand in hand with socialization, so your puppy will be learning how to walk on a lead at the same time that he's meeting the neighborhood. Because the English Toy Spaniel is such a terrific breed, everyone will enjoy meeting "the new kid on the block." Take him for short walks to the park and to other dog-friendly places where he will encounter new people, especially children. Puppies automatically recognize children as "little people" and are drawn to play with them. Just make sure that you supervise these meetings and that the children do not get too rough or encourage him to play too hard. An overzealous pup can often nip too hard, frightening the child and in turn making the puppy overly excited. A bad experience in puppyhood can impact a dog for life, so a pup that has a negative experience with a child may grow up to be shy or even aggressive around children.

Take your puppy along on your daily errands. Puppies are natural "people magnets," and most people who see your pup will want to pet him. All of these encounters will help to mold him into a confident adult dog. Likewise, you will soon feel like a confident, responsible dog owner, rightly proud of your mannerly English Toy Spaniel.

TOXIC PLANTS

Plants are natural puppy magnets, but many can be harmful, even fatal, if ingested by a puppy or adult dog. Scout your yard and home interior and remove any plants, bushes or flowers that could be even mildly dangerous. It could save your puppy's life. You can obtain a complete list of toxic plants from your veterinarian, at the public library or by looking online.

If you have your pup before he is ten weeks old, be especially careful of his encounters and experiences through ten weeks of age. The time between eight and ten weeks is called the "fear period." This is a serious imprinting period, and all contact during this time should be gentle and positive. A frightening or negative event could leave a permanent impression that could affect his future behavior if a similar situation arises.

Also make sure that your puppy has received his first and second rounds of vaccinations before you expose him to other dogs or bring him to places that other dogs may frequent. Avoid dog parks and other strange-dog areas until your vet assures you that your puppy is fully immunized and resistant to the diseases that can be passed between canines. Discuss safe socialization with your breeder, as some breeders recommend socializing the puppy even before he has received all of his inoculations, depending on how outgoing the puppy may be.

LEADER OF THE PUPPY'S PACK

Like other canines, your puppy needs an authority figure, someone he can look up to and regard as the leader of his "pack." His first pack leader was his dam, who taught him to be polite and

> **COST OF OWNERSHIP**
> The purchase price of your puppy is merely the first expense in the typical dog budget. Quality dog food, veterinary care (sickness and health maintenance), dog supplies and grooming costs will add up to big bucks every year. Can you adequately afford to support a canine addition to the family?

not chew too hard on her ears or nip at her muzzle. He learned those same lessons from his littermates. If he played too rough, they cried in pain and stopped the game, which sent an important message to the rowdy puppy.

As puppies play together, they are also struggling to determine who will be the boss. Being pack animals, dogs need someone to be in charge. If a litter of puppies remained together beyond puppyhood, one of the pups would emerge as the strongest one, the one who calls the shots.

Once your puppy leaves the pack, he will look intuitively for a new leader. If he does not recognize you as that leader, he will try to assume that position for himself. Of course, it is hard to imagine your adorable English Toy Spaniel puppy trying to be in charge when he is so small and seemingly helpless. You must remember that these are natural canine instincts. Do not cave in

Dinner with a friend. The breeder weans the pups onto a quality diet and will advise you about proper feeding for your new puppy.

and allow your pup to get the upper "paw"!

Just as socialization is so important during these first 20 weeks, so too is your puppy's early education. He was born without any bad habits. He does not know what is good or bad behavior. If he does things like nipping and digging, it's because he is having fun and doesn't know that humans consider these things as "bad." It's your job to teach him proper puppy manners, and this is the best time to accomplish that—before he has developed bad habits, since it is much more difficult to "unlearn" or correct unacceptable learned behavior than to teach good behavior from the start.

Make sure that all members of the family understand the importance of being consistent when training their new puppy. If you tell the puppy to stay off the sofa and your daughter allows him to cuddle on the couch to watch her favorite television show, your pup will be confused about what he is and is not allowed to do. Have a family conference before your pup comes home so that everyone understands the basic principles of puppy training and the rules you have set forth for the pup, and agrees to follow them.

The old saying that "an ounce of prevention is worth a pound of cure" is especially true when it comes to puppies. It is much easier to prevent inappropriate behavior than it is to change it. It's also easier and less stressful for the pup, since it will keep discipline to a minimum and create a more positive learning environment for him. That, in turn, will also be easier on you.

Here are a few commonsense tips to keep your belongings safe and your puppy out of trouble:

- Keep your closet doors closed and your shoes, socks and other apparel off the floor so your puppy can't get to them.
- Keep a secure lid on the trash container or put the trash where your puppy can't dig into it. He can't damage what he can't reach!
- Supervise your puppy at all times to make sure he is not getting into mischief. If he starts

BE CONSISTENT

Consistency is a key element, in fact is absolutely necessary, to a puppy's learning environment. A behavior (such as chewing, jumping up or climbing onto the furniture) cannot be forbidden one day and then allowed the next. That will only confuse the pup, and he will not understand what he is supposed to do. Just one or two episodes of allowing an undesirable behavior to "slide" will imprint that behavior on a puppy's brain and make that behavior more difficult to erase or change.

Every pup needs the opportunity to explore, so give your curious spaniel time to get acquainted with his new home, indoors and out, under your watchful eye.

to chew the corner of the rug, you can distract him instantly by tossing a toy for him to fetch. You also will be able to whisk him outside when you notice that he is about to piddle on the carpet. If you can't see your puppy, you can't teach him or correct his behavior.

SOLVING PUPPY PROBLEMS

CHEWING AND NIPPING

Nipping at fingers and toes is normal puppy behavior. Chewing is also the way that puppies investigate their surroundings. However, you will have to teach your puppy that chewing anything other than his toys is not acceptable. That won't happen overnight and at times puppy teeth will test your patience. However, if you allow

nipping and chewing to continue, just think about the damage that a mature English Toy Spaniel can do with a full set of adult teeth.

Whenever your puppy nips your hand or fingers, cry out "Ouch!" in a loud voice, which should startle your puppy and stop him from nipping, even if only for a moment. Immediately distract him by offering a small treat or an appropriate toy for him to chew instead (which means having chew toys and puppy treats handy or in your pockets at all times). Praise him when he takes the toy and tell him what a good fellow he is. Praise is just as or even more important in puppy training as discipline and correction.

Puppies also tend to nip at children more often than adults, since they perceive little ones to be more vulnerable and more similar to their littermates. Teach your children appropriate responses to nipping behavior. If they are unable to handle it themselves, you may have to intervene. Puppy nips can be quite painful and a child's fright-ened reaction will only encour-age a puppy to nip harder, which is a natural canine response. As with all other puppy situations, interaction between your English Toy Spaniel puppy and children should be supervised.

Chewing on objects, not just

family members' fingers and ankles, is also normal canine behavior that can be especially tedious (for the owner, not the pup) during the teething period when the puppy's adult teeth are coming in. At this stage, chewing just plain feels good. Furniture legs and cabinet corners are common puppy favorites. Shoes and other personal items also taste pretty good to a pup.

The best solution is, once again, prevention. If you value something, keep it tucked away and out of reach. You can't hide your dining-room table in a closet, but you can try to deflect the chewing by applying a bitter product made just to deter dogs from chewing. This spray-on substance is vile-tasting, although safe for dogs, and most puppies will avoid the forbidden object after one tiny taste. You also can apply the product to your leather leash if the puppy tries to chew on his lead during leash-training sessions.

Keep a ready supply of safe chews handy to offer your English Toy Spaniel as a distraction when he starts to chew on something that's a "no-no." Remember, at this tender age he does not yet know what is permitted or forbidden, so you have to be "on call" every minute he's awake and on the prowl.

You may lose a treasure or two during your puppy's growing-

THE FAMILY FELINE

A resident cat has feline squatter's rights. The cat will treat the newcomer (your puppy) as she sees fit, regardless of what you do or say. So it's best to let the two of them work things out on their own terms. Cats have a height advantage and will generally leap to higher ground to avoid direct contact with a rambunctious pup. Some will hiss and boldly swat at a pup who passes by or tries to reach the cat. Keep the puppy under control in the presence of the cat and they will eventually become accustomed to each other.

Here's a hint: move the cat's litter box where the puppy can't get into it! It's best to do so well before the pup comes home so the cat is used to the new location.

up period, and the furniture could sustain a nasty nick or two. These can be trying times, so be prepared for those inevitable accidents and comfort yourself in knowing that this too shall pass.

JUMPING UP

Although English Toy Spaniel pups are not known to be notorious jumpers, they are still puppies after all, and puppies jump up—on you, your guests, your counters and your furniture. Just another normal part of growing up, and one you need to meet head-on before it becomes an ingrained habit.

The key to jump correction is consistency. You cannot correct your English Toy Spaniel for jumping up on you today, then allow it to happen tomorrow by greeting him with hugs and kisses. As you have learned by now, consistency is critical to all puppy lessons.

For starters, try turning your back as soon as the puppy jumps. Jumping up is a means of gaining your attention and, if the pup can't see your face, he may get discouraged and learn that he loses eye contact with his beloved master when he jumps up.

Leash corrections also work, and most puppies respond well to a leash tug if they jump. Grasp the leash close to the puppy's collar and give a quick tug downward, using the command "Off." Do not use the word "Down," since "Down" is used to teach the puppy to lie down, which is a separate action that he will learn during his education in the basic commands. As soon as the puppy has backed off, tell him to sit and immediately praise him for doing so. This will take many repeti-

MEET AND MINGLE

Puppies need to meet people and see the world if they are to grow up confident and unafraid. Take your puppy with you on everyday outings and errands. On-lead walks around the neighborhood and to the park offer the pup good exposure to the goings-on of his new human world. Avoid areas frequented by other dogs until your puppy has had his full round of puppy shots; ask your vet when your pup will be properly protected. Arrange for your puppy to meet new people of all ages every week.

tions and won't be accomplished quickly, so don't get discouraged or give up; you must be even more persistent than your puppy.

Another method used for jump correction is the spritzer bottle. Fill a spray bottle with water mixed with a bit of lemon juice or vinegar. As soon as the puppy jumps, command him "Off" and spritz him with the water mixture. Of course, that means having the spray bottle handy whenever or wherever jumping usually happens.

Yet another method to discourage jumping is grasping the puppy's paws and holding them gently but firmly until he struggles to get away. Wait a brief moment or two, then release his paws and give him a command to sit. He should eventually learn that jumping gets him into an uncomfortable predicament.

Children are major victims of puppy jumping, since puppies view little people as ready targets for jumping up as well as nipping. If your children (or their friends) are unable to dispense jump corrections, you will have to intervene and handle it for them.

Important to prevention is also knowing what you should not do. Never kick your English Toy Spaniel (for any reason, not just for jumping) or knock him in the chest with your leg. That maneuver could actually harm your puppy. Vets can tell you stories about puppies who suffered broken bones after being banged about when they jumped up.

Puppy Whining

Puppies often cry and whine, just as infants and little children do. It's their way of telling us that they are lonely or in need of attention. Your puppy will miss

TEMPERAMENT ABOVE ALL ELSE

Regardless of breed, a puppy's disposition is perhaps his most important quality. It is, after all, what makes a puppy lovable and "livable." If the puppy's parents or grandparents are known to be snappy or aggressive, the puppy is likely to inherit those tendencies. That can lead to serious problems, such as the dog's becoming a biter, which can lead to eventual abandonment.

A soft, warm bed and toys to keep him occupied are among the things that will make your pup's transition to his new home as stress-free as possible.

his littermates and will feel insecure when he is left alone. You may be out of the house or just in another room, but he will still feel alone. During these times, the puppy's crate should be his personal comfort station, a place all his own where he can feel safe and secure. Once he learns that being alone is okay and not something to be feared, he will settle down without crying or objecting. You might want to leave a radio on while he is crated, as the sound of human voices can be soothing and will give the impression that people are around.

Give your puppy a favorite cuddly toy or chew toy to entertain him whenever he is crated. You will both be happier: the puppy because he is safe in his den and you because he is quiet, safe and not getting into puppy escapades that can wreak havoc

in your house or cause him danger.

To make sure that your puppy will always view his crate as a safe and cozy place, never, ever use the crate as punishment. That's the best way to turn the crate into a negative place that the pup will want to avoid. Sure, you can use the crate for your own peace of mind if your puppy is getting into trouble and needs some "time out." Just don't let him know that! Never scold the pup and immediately place him into the crate. Count to ten, give him a couple of hugs and maybe a treat, then scoot him into his crate.

It's also important not to make a big fuss when he is released from the crate. That will make getting out of the crate more appealing than being in the crate, which is just the opposite of what you are trying to achieve.

HAPPY PUPPIES COME RUNNING

Never call your puppy (or adult dog) to come to you and then scold him or discipline him when he gets there. He will make a natural association between coming to you and being scolded, and he will think he was a bad dog for coming to you. He will then be reluctant to come whenever he is called. Always praise your puppy every time he comes to you.

ENGLISH TOY SPANIEL

Adding an English Toy Spaniel to your household means adding a new family member who will need your care each and every day. When your English Toy pup first comes home, you will start a routine with him so that, as he grows up, your dog will have a daily schedule just as you do. The aspects of your dog's daily care will likewise become regular parts of your day, so you'll both have a new schedule. Dogs learn by consistency and thrive on routine: regular times for meals, exercise, grooming and potty trips are just as important for your dog as they are for you. Your dog's schedule will depend much on your family's daily routine, but remember that you now have a new member of the family who is part of your day every day.

FEEDING

Feeding your dog the best diet is based on various factors, including age, activity level, overall condition and size of breed. When you visit the breeder, he will share with you his advice about the proper diet for your dog based on his experience with the breed and the foods with which he has

> ### VARIETY IS THE SPICE
> Although dog-food manufacturers contend that dogs don't like variety in their diets, studies show quite the opposite to be true. Dogs would much rather vary their meals than eat the same old chow day in and day out. Dry kibble is no more exciting for a dog than the same bowl of bran flakes would be for you. Fortunately, there are dozens of varieties available on the market, and your dog will likely show preference for certain flavors over others. A word of warning: don't overdo it or you'll develop a fussy eater who only prefers chopped beef fillet and asparagus tips every night.

had success. Likewise, your vet will be a helpful source of advice throughout the dog's life and will aid you in planning a diet for optimal health.

FEEDING THE PUPPY

Of course, your pup's very first food will be his dam's milk. There may be special situations in which pups fail to nurse, necessitating that the breeder hand-feed

SWITCHING FOODS

There are certain times in a dog's life when it becomes necessary to switch his food; for example, from puppy to adult food and then from adult to senior-dog food. Additionally, you may decide to feed your pup a different type of food from what he received from the breeder, and there may be "emergency" situations in which you can't find your dog's normal brand and have to offer something else temporarily. Anytime a change is made, for whatever reason, the switch must be done gradually. You don't want to upset the dog's stomach or end up with a picky eater who refuses to eat something new. A tried-and-true approach is, over the course of about a week, to mix a little of the new food in with the old, increasing the proportion of new to old as the days progress. At the end of the week, you'll be feeding his regular portions of the new food, and he will barely notice the change.

them with a formula, but for the most part pups spend the first weeks of life nursing from their dam. The breeder weans the pups by gradually introducing solid foods and decreasing the milk meals. Pups may even start themselves off on the weaning process, albeit inadvertently, if they snatch bites from their mom's food bowl.

By the time the pups are ready for new homes, they are fully weaned and eating a good puppy food. As a new owner, you may be thinking, "Great! The breeder has taken care of the hard part." Not so fast.

A puppy's first year of life is the time when all or most of his growth and development takes place. This is a delicate time, and diet plays a huge role in proper skeletal and muscular formation. Improper diet and exercise habits can lead to damaging problems that will compromise the dog's health and movement for his entire life. That being said, new owners should not worry needlessly. With the myriad types of food formulated specifically for growing pups of different-sized breeds, dog-food manufacturers have taken much of the guesswork out of feeding your puppy well. Since growth-food formulas are designed to provide the nutrition that a growing puppy needs, it is unnecessary and, in fact, can prove harmful to add supplements to the diet. Research has shown that too much of certain vitamin supplements and minerals predispose a dog to skeletal problems. It's by no means a case of "if a little is good, a lot is better." At every stage of your dog's life, too much or too little in the way of nutrients can be harmful, which is why a manufactured complete food is the easiest way to know that your dog is getting what he needs.

Because of a young pup's small body and accordingly small digestive system, his daily portion will be divided up into small meals throughout the day. This can mean starting off with three or more meals a day and decreasing the number of meals as the pup matures. Eventually you can feed only one meal a day, although it is generally thought that dividing the day's food into two meals on a morning/evening schedule is healthier for the dog's digestion.

Regarding the feeding schedule, feeding the pup at the same times and in the same place each day is important for both housebreaking purposes and establishing the dog's everyday routine. As for the amount to feed, growing puppies generally need proportionately more food per body weight than their adult counterparts, but a pup should never be allowed to gain excess weight. Dogs of all ages should be kept in proper body condition, but extra weight can strain a pup's developing frame, causing skeletal problems.

Watch your pup's weight as he grows and, if the recommended amounts seem to be too much or too little for your pup, consult the vet about appropriate dietary changes. Keep in mind that treats, although small, can quickly add up throughout the day, contributing unnecessary calories. Treats are fine when used prudently; opt for dog treats specially formulated to be healthy or for nutritious snacks like small pieces of cheese or cooked chicken.

NOT HUNGRY?

No dog in his right mind would turn down his dinner, would he? If you notice that your dog has lost interest in his food, there could be any number of causes. Dental problems are a common cause of appetite loss, one that is often overlooked. If your dog has a toothache, a loose tooth or sore gums from infection, chances are it doesn't feel so good to chew. Think about when you've had a toothache! If your dog does not approach the food bowl with his usual enthusiasm, look inside his mouth for signs of a problem. Whatever the cause, you'll want to consult your vet so that your chow hound can get back to his happy, hungry self as soon as possible.

FEEDING THE ADULT DOG

For the adult (meaning physically mature) dog, feeding properly is about maintenance, not growth. A Charlie can be changed to an

JUST ADD MEAT

An organic alternative to the traditional dog kibble or canned food comes in the form of grain-based feeds. These dry cereal-type products consist of oat and rye flakes, corn meal, wheat germ, dried kelp and other natural ingredients. The manufacturers recommend that the food be mixed with fresh meat in a ratio of two parts grain to one part meat. As an alternative to fresh meat, investigate freeze-dried meat and fermented meat products, which makers claim are more nutritious and digestible for dogs.

adult diet at about eight months of age. Again, correct weight is a concern. Your dog should appear fit and should have an evident "waist." His ribs should not be protruding (a sign of being underweight), but they should be covered by only a slight layer of fat. Under normal circumstances, an adult dog can be maintained fairly easily with a high-quality nutritionally complete adult-formula food.

Factor treats into your dog's overall daily caloric intake, and avoid offering table scraps. Overweight dogs are more prone to health problems. Research has even shown that obesity takes years off a dog's life. With that in mind, resist the urge to overfeed and over-treat. Don't make unnec-

essary additions to your dog's diet, whether with tidbits or with extra vitamins and minerals.

The amount of food needed for proper maintenance will vary depending on the individual dog's activity level, but you will be able to tell whether the daily portions are keeping him in good shape. With the wide variety of good complete foods available, choosing what to feed is largely a matter of personal preference. Just as with the puppy, the adult dog should have consistency in his mealtimes and feeding place. In addition to a consistent routine, regular mealtimes also allow the owner to see how much his dog is eating. If the dog seems never to be satisfied or, likewise, becomes uninterested in his food, the owner will know right away that something is wrong and can consult the vet.

DIETS FOR THE AGING DOG

A good rule of thumb is that once a dog has reached 75% of his expected lifespan, he has reached "senior citizen" or geriatric status. Your English Toy Spaniel will be considered a senior at about 8 years of age; based on his size, he has a projected lifespan of about 10–15 years. (The smallest breeds generally enjoy the longest lives and the largest breeds the shortest.)

What does aging have to do with your dog's diet? No, he won't get a discount at the local diner's

early-bird special. Yes, he will require some dietary changes to accommodate the changes that come along with increased age. One change is that the older dog's dietary needs become more similar to that of a puppy. Specifically, dogs can metabolize more protein as youngsters and seniors than in the adult-maintenance stage. Discuss with your vet whether you need to switch to a higher-protein or senior-formulated food or whether your current adult-dog

DIET DON'TS

- Got milk? Don't give it to your dog! Dogs cannot tolerate large quantities of cows' milk, as they do not have the enzymes to digest lactose.
- You may have heard of dog owners who add raw eggs to their dogs' food for a shiny coat or to make the food more palatable, but consumption of raw eggs too often can cause a deficiency of the vitamin biotin.
- Avoid feeding table scraps, as they will upset the balance of the dog's complete food. Additionally, fatty or highly seasoned foods can cause upset canine stomachs.
- Do not offer raw meat to your dog. Raw meat can contain parasites; it also is high in fat.
- Vitamin A toxicity in dogs can be caused by too much raw liver, especially if the dog already gets enough vitamin A in his balanced diet, which should be the case.
- Bones like chicken, pork chop and other soft bones are not suitable, as they easily splinter.

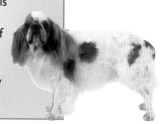

THE BOVINE CANINE

Does your dog's grazing in the back yard have you wondering whether he's actually a farm animal in disguise? Many owners have noticed their dogs eating grass and wonder why. It is thought that dogs might eat grass to settle their stomachs or to relieve upset tummies. Even cats have been known to eat grass for the same reasons! Stomach upset can be caused by various things, including poor digestion and parasites.

Unfortunately, while the grass may make the dog feel better very temporarily, often they vomit shortly after eating it, as grass can be irritating to a dog's stomach lining. Even worse, who knows what he is ingesting along with the grass? He could be swallowing insects, germs or parasites, thus perpetuating the problem. Grass-eating should be discouraged when you catch the dog in the act, and a trip to the vet to determine the underlying cause is in order.

food contains sufficient nutrition for the senior.

Watching the dog's weight remains essential, even more so in the senior stage. Older dogs are already more vulnerable to illness, and obesity only contributes to their susceptibility to problems. As the older dog becomes less active and thus exercises less, his regular portions may cause him to gain weight. At this point, you may consider decreasing his daily food intake or switching to a reduced-calorie food. As with other changes, you should consult your vet for advice.

DON'T FORGET THE WATER!

For a dog, it's always time for a drink! Regardless of what type of food he eats, there's no doubt that he needs plenty of water. Fresh cold water, in a clean bowl, should be freely available to your dog at all times. There are special circumstances, such as during puppy housebreaking, when you will want to monitor your pup's water intake so that you will be able to predict when he will need to relieve himself, but water must be available to him nonetheless. Water is essential for hydration and proper body function just as it is in humans.

You will get to know how much your dog typically drinks in a day. Of course, in the heat or if exercising vigorously, he will be more thirsty and will drink

QUENCHING HIS THIRST

Is your dog drinking more than normal and trying to lap up everything in sight? Excessive drinking has many different causes. Obvious causes for a dog's being thirstier than usual are hot weather and vigorous exercise. However, if your dog is drinking more for no apparent reason, you could have cause for concern. Serious conditions like kidney or liver disease, diabetes and various types of hormonal problems can all be indicated by excessive drinking. If you notice your dog's being excessively thirsty, contact your vet at once. Hopefully there will be a simpler explanation, but the earlier a serious problem is detected, the sooner it can be treated, with a better rate of cure.

more. However, if he begins to drink noticeably more water for no apparent reason, this could signal any of various problems, and you are advised to consult your vet.

Water is the best drink for dogs. Some owners are tempted to give milk from time to time or to moisten dry food with milk, but dogs do not have the enzymes necessary to digest the lactose in milk, which is much different from the milk that nursing puppies receive. Therefore stick with clean fresh water to quench your dog's thirst, and always have it readily available to him.

EXERCISE

It's fair to say that the English Toy Spaniel requires less exercise than all of the other spaniels! Toy dogs, by and large, are more prone to sitting on laps than running them. Nevertheless, some form of exercise is a basic requirement of life. A sedentary lifestyle is as harmful to a dog as it is to a person.

Given the breed's short legs and delicate structure, the English Toy Spaniel gets a good bit of his exercise moving around the home and yard. Yet a nice walk outdoors on lead is enjoyable and healthy for both of you. Brisk walks, once the puppy reaches three or four months of age, will stimulate heart rates and build muscle for both dog and owner. As the dog reaches adulthood, the speed and distance of the walks can be increased as long as they are kept reasonable and comfortable for both of you.

Play sessions in the yard and letting the dog run free in a safely enclosed outdoor area, under your supervision, also are good forms of exercise for the English Toy Spaniel. Fetching games can be played indoors or out; these are excellent for giving your dog active play that he will enjoy. Chasing things that move comes

Don't let the "toy" fool you. This is an alert little spaniel with enough hunting instinct to set him off and running. He must be on leash when in an open area.

naturally to dogs of all breeds, especially spaniels. When your English Toy Spaniel runs after the ball or object, praise him for picking it up and encourage him to bring it back to you for another throw. Never go to the object and pick it up yourself, or you'll soon find that you are the one retrieving the objects rather than the dog! If you choose to play games outdoors, you must have a securely fenced-in yard and/or have the dog attached to at least a 25-foot light line for security. You want your Charlie to run, but not run away!

Bear in mind that an overweight dog should never be suddenly over-exercised; instead he should be encouraged to increase exercise slowly. Not only is exercise essential to keep the dog's body fit, it is essential to his mental well-being. A bored dog will find something to do, which often manifests itself in some type of destructive behavior. In this sense, exercise is essential for the owner's mental well-being as well.

GROOMING YOUR ENGLISH TOY SPANIEL

Do understand before purchasing your dog that this is a breed with a coat that needs maintenance, although, fortunately, the English Toy is quite low-maintenance compared to most of the other toy breeds. Grooming is a must, whether you have a dog for the show ring or one that is a household pet. Think of it in terms of your child—you bathe your youngster, comb his hair and put a clean set of clothes on him. The end product is that you have a child that smells good and looks nice, and that you enjoy having in

PUPPY STEPS

Puppies are brimming with activity and enthusiasm. It seems that they can play all day and night without tiring, but don't overdo your puppy's exercise regimen. Easy does it for the puppy's first six to nine months. Keep walks brief and don't let the puppy engage in stressful jumping games. The puppy frame is delicate, and too much exercise during those critical growing months can cause injury to his bone structure, ligaments and musculature. Save his first jog for his first birthday!

your company. It is the same with your English Toy—keep the dog brushed, combed and cleaned, and you will find it a pleasure to be in his company.

Grooming is very fundamental with this breed. Despite their long coats, English Toys are more-or-less "wash-and-go" dogs, although special care must be taken to keep the coat mat-free. The long feathering is most prone to mats and tangles; this includes the ears and ear area, the "armpits," the backs of the legs and the tail and surrounding area. Routine grooming should consist of a weekly brushing and combing, and bathing as needed, which will be probably about every few weeks. If you encounter a mat in the coat, try to separate it gently with your fingers. In the worst cases, you may need to cut the mat out, but it is better for the coat to untangle it yourself. Be gentle when combing through the feathering; the areas most prone to mats are also the most sensitive, and you do not want grooming to be a painful experience for your English Toy. This is not a breed that should be trimmed, although you should cut away excess hair between the toes and you may want to trim around the genital area for cleanliness.

Of course, you can eliminate all of the grooming for yourself, except for the weekly brushing, if you take your dog to the groomer every three months. However, many pet owners like to spend the time with their pets and, do

TWO'S COMPANY

One surefire method of increasing your adult dog's exercise plan is to adopt a second dog. If your dog is well socialized, he should take to his new canine pal in no time and soon the two will be giving each other lots of activity and exercise as they play, romp and explore together. Most owners agree that two dogs are hardly much more work than one. If you cannot afford a second dog, get together with a friend or neighbor who has a well-trained dog. Your dog will definitely enjoy the company of a new four-legged playmate.

remember, many pet owners do a much better job grooming their dogs than some professional groomers. With routine grooming, you will have a happy, clean and good-smelling English Toy Spaniel who will look nice and tidy, and whom you will be happy to take out in public.

BATHING

In general, your pet English Toy Spaniel should be bathed every few weeks, possibly more often if he gets into something messy or if he starts to smell like a dog. Show dogs are usually bathed before every show, which could be as frequent as weekly, although this depends on the owner. Bathing too frequently can have negative effects on the skin and coat, removing natural oils and causing dryness.

If you give your dog his first bath when he is young, he will become accustomed to the process. Wrestling a dog into the tub or chasing a freshly shampooed dog who has escaped from the bath will be no fun! Most dogs don't naturally enjoy their baths, but you at least want yours to cooperate with you.

Before bathing the dog, have the items you'll need close at hand. First decide where you will bathe the dog. You should have a tub or basin with a non-slip surface. Your English Toy can even be bathed in a sink. In warm weather, some like to use a portable pool in the yard, although you'll want to make sure your dog doesn't head for the nearest dirt pile following his bath! You will

PUPPY LE PEW

On that ill-fated day when your puppy insults the neighborhood skunk by calling him a weasel, you will likely have the unhappy chore of "de-skunking" your dog. Skunks are not afraid of puppies (or even full-sized dogs) and will take on an approaching "predator." The skunk's spray is a nasty compound called thiols, a thick, oily liquid that can also be found in decaying flesh or feces. After the skunk hisses, growls and does his "don't-mess-with-me" dance, he sprays the unsuspecting canine.

The age-old remedy was to bathe a "skunked" dog in tomato juice, but thanks to chemist Paul Krebaum, you can put away your can opener. Krebaum provides us with this easy and effective recipe to deodorize your stinky puppy: 1 quart 3% hydrogen peroxide; 1/4 cup baking soda; and 1 teaspoon liquid dish detergent. Work the soapy formula into the dog's coat and keep it out of the dog's eyes. Rinse the dog thoroughly after the bath. Do not make this formula and attempt to bottle it—it will explode!

Incidentally, the skunk is in fact in the weasel family, but there's no sense arguing with the nasty-tempered mouse-eating fellow.

WATER SHORTAGE

No matter how well behaved your dog is, bathing is always a project! Nothing can substitute for a good warm bath, but owners do have the option of giving their dogs "dry" baths. Pet shops sell excellent products, in both powder and spray forms, designed for spot-cleaning your dog. These dry shampoos are convenient for touch-up jobs when you don't have the time to bathe your dog in the traditional way.

Muddy feet, messy behinds and smelly coats can be spot-cleaned and deodorized with a "wet-nap"-style cleaner. On those days when your dog insists on rolling in fresh goose droppings and there's no time for a bath, a spot bath can save the day. These pre-moistened wipes are also handy for other grooming needs like wiping faces, ears and eyes and freshening tails and behinds.

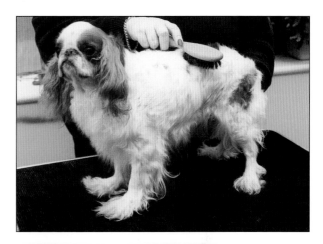

ABOVE: Use a grooming table with a non-skid surface, adjusted to a proper height. A bristle brush can be used on the body coat. LEFT: A fine-toothed comb can be used gently on the long ear feathering.

also need a hose or shower spray to wet the coat thoroughly, a shampoo formulated for dogs, absorbent towels and a blow dryer. Human shampoos are too harsh for dogs' coats and will dry them out.

Before wetting the dog, give him a brush-through to remove any dead hair, dirt and mats. Make sure he is at ease in the tub and have the water at a comfortable temperature. Begin bathing by wetting the coat all the way down

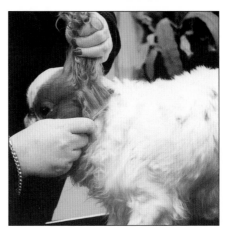

Don't forget under the ears. Out-of-the-way areas tend to mat more easily and are more sensitive, so always use a gentle touch.

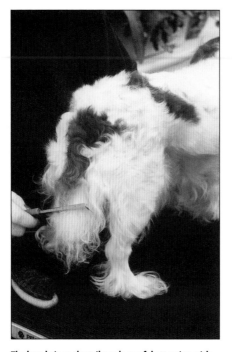

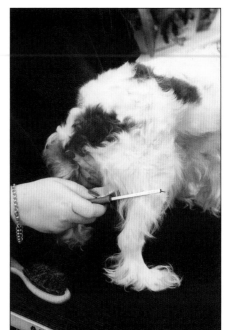

The long hair on the tail needs careful attention with the comb, as it can become tangled easily.

Feathering on the legs also benefits from attention with the fine-toothed comb.

Keep your English Toy's eye area and face clean by wiping gently with a damp cloth.

Use grooming time to clean the dog's ears. Using a cotton swab, shown here, can be dangerous as you can accidentally poke into the ear and cause injury.

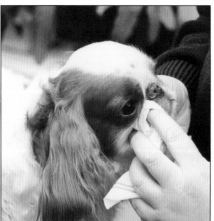

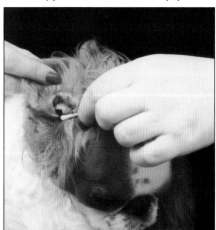

to the skin. Massage in the shampoo, keeping it away from his face and eyes. Rinse him thoroughly, again avoiding the eyes and ears, as you don't want to get water into the ear canals. A thorough rinsing

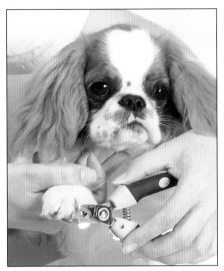

Your pet shop sells different styles of nail clippers. Select a sturdy, efficient one for your English Toy.

is important, as shampoo residue is drying and itchy to the dog. After rinsing, wrap him in a towel to absorb the initial moisture; do not rub the coat. Finish drying with a blow dryer on low heat, held at a safe distance from the dog and brushing as you dry. You should keep the dog indoors and away from drafts until he is completely dry.

NAIL CLIPPING

Having their nails trimmed is not on many dogs' lists of favorite things to do. With this in mind, you will need to accustom your puppy to the procedure at a young age so that he will sit still (well, as still as he can) for his pedicures. Long nails can cause the dog's feet to spread, which is not good for him; likewise, long nails can hurt if they unintentionally

THE MONTHLY GRIND

If your dog doesn't like the feeling of nail clippers or if you're not comfortable using them, you may wish to try an electric nail grinder. This tool has a small sandpaper disc on the end that rotates to grind the nails down. Some feel that using a grinder reduces the risk of cutting into the quick; this can be true if the tool is used properly. Usually you will be able to tell where the quick is before you get to it. A benefit of the grinder is that it creates a smooth finish on the nails so that there are no ragged edges.

Because the tool makes noise, your dog should be introduced to it before the actual grinding takes place. Turn it on and let your dog hear the noise; turn it off and let him inspect it with you holding it. Use the grinder gently, holding it firmly and progressing a little at a time until you reach the proper length. Look at the nail as you grind so that you do not go too short. Stop at any indication that you are nearing the quick. It will take a few sessions for both you and the puppy to get used to the grinder. Make sure that you don't let his hair get tangled in the grinder!

scratch, not good for you.

Some dogs' nails are worn down naturally by regular walking on hard surfaces, so the frequency with which you clip depends on your individual dog. Look at his nails from time to time and clip as needed; a good way to know when it's time for a trim is if you hear your dog clicking as he walks across the floor.

There are several types of nail clippers and even electric nail-grinding tools made for dogs; first we'll discuss using the clipper. To start, have your clipper ready and some doggie treats on hand. You want your pup to view his nail-clipping sessions in a positive light, and what better way to convince him than with food? You may want to enlist the help of an assistant to comfort the pup and offer treats as you concentrate on the clipping itself. The guillotine-type clipper is thought of by many as the easiest type to use; the nail tip is inserted into the opening, and blades on the top and bottom snip it off in one clip.

Start by grasping the pup's paw; a little pressure on the foot pad causes the nail to extend, making it easier to clip. Clip off a little at a time. If you can see the "quick," which is a blood vessel that runs through each nail, you will know how much to trim, as you do not want to cut into the quick. On that note, if you do cut the quick, which will cause bleed-ing, you can stem the flow of blood with a styptic pencil or other clot-ting agent. If you mistakenly nip the quick, do not panic or fuss, as this will cause the pup to be afraid. Simply reassure the pup, stop the bleeding and move on to the next nail. Don't be discouraged; you will become a professional canine pedicurist with practice.

You may or may not be able to see the quick, so it's best to just clip off a small bit at a time. If you see a dark dot in the center of the nail, this is the quick and your cue to stop clipping. Tell the puppy he's a "good boy" and offer a piece of treat with each nail. You can also use nail-clipping time to examine the footpads, making sure that they are not dry and cracked and that nothing has become embedded in them.

The nail grinder, the other choice, is many owners' first choice. Accustoming the puppy to the sound of the grinder and sensa-tion of the buzz presents fewer challenges than the clipper, and there's no chance of cutting through the quick. Use the grinder on a low setting and always talk soothingly to your dog. He won't mind his salon visit, and he'll have nicely polished nails as well.

EAR CLEANING

While keeping your dog's ears clean unfortunately will not cause him to "hear" your commands any better, it will protect him from ear infection and ear-mite infestation. In addition, a dog's ears are vulnerable to waxy build-up and to collecting foreign matter from the outdoors. Look in your dog's ears regularly to ensure that they look pink, clean and otherwise healthy. Even if they look fine, an odor in the ears signals a problem and means it's time to call the vet.

A dog's ears should be cleaned regularly; once a week is suggested, and you can do this along with your regular brushing. The English Toy's pendulous ears should be kept clean with a cotton wipe and ear powder made especially for dogs. Using a cotton ball or pad, and never probing into the ear canal, wipe the ear gently. You can use an ear-cleansing liquid or powder available from your vet or pet-supply store; alternatively, you might prefer to use home-made solutions with ingredients like white vinegar or hydrogen peroxide diluted with water. Ask your vet about home remedies before you attempt to concoct something on your own!

Keep your dog's ears free of excess hair by plucking it as needed. If done gently, this will be painless for the dog. Look for wax, brown droppings (a sign of ear mites), redness or any other abnormalities. At the first sign of a problem, contact your vet so that he can prescribe an appropriate medication.

EYE CARE

During grooming sessions, pay extra attention to the condition of your dog's eyes. If the area around the eyes is soiled or if tear staining has occurred, there are various cleaning agents made especially

PRESERVING THOSE PEARLY WHITES

What do you treasure more than the smile of your beloved canine pal? Brushing your dog's teeth is just as important as brushing your own. Neglecting your dog's teeth can lead to tooth loss, periodontal disease and inflamed gums, not to mention bad breath. Can you find the time to brush your dog's teeth every day? If not, you should do so once a week at the very least, though every day is truly the ideal. Your vet should give your dog a thorough dental examination during his annual check-ups.

Pet shops sell terrific tooth-care devices, including specially designed toothbrushes, yummy toothpastes and finger-model brushes. You can use a human toothbrush with soft bristles, but never use human toothpastes, which can damage the dog's enamel. Baking soda is an alternative to doggie toothpastes, but your dog will be more receptive to canine toothpastes with the flavor of liver or hamburger. Make tooth care fun for your dog. Let him think that you're "horsing around" with his mouth. When brushing the dog's teeth, begin with the largest teeth (the canines) and proceed back toward the molars.

for this purpose. Look at the dog's eyes to make sure no debris has entered; dogs with large eyes and those who spend time outdoors are especially prone to this.

The signs of an eye infection are obvious: mucus, redness, puffiness, scabs or other signs of irritation. If your dog's eyes become infected, the vet will likely prescribe an antibiotic ointment for treatment. If you notice signs of more serious problems, such as opacities in the eye, which usually indicate cataracts, consult the vet at once. Taking time to pay attention to your dog's eyes will alert you in the early stages of any problem so that you can get your dog treatment as soon as possible. You could save your dog's sight!

IDENTIFICATION

You love your English Toy Spaniel and want to keep him safe. Of course you take every precaution to prevent his escaping from the yard or becoming lost or stolen. You have a sturdy high fence and you always keep your dog on lead when out and about in public places. If your dog is not properly identified, however, you are overlooking a major aspect of his safety. We hope to never be in a situation where our dog is missing, but we should practice prevention in the unfortunate case that this happens; identification greatly increases the chances of your dog's being returned to you.

There are several ways to identify your dog. First, the traditional dog tag should be a staple in your dog's wardrobe, attached to his everyday collar. Tags can be made of sturdy plastic and various metals and should include your contact information so that a person who finds the dog can get in touch with you right away to arrange his return. Many people today enjoy the wide range of decorative tags available, so have fun and create a tag to match your dog's personality. Of course, it is important that the tag stays on the collar, so have a secure "O" ring attachment; you also can explore the type of tag that slides right onto the collar.

In addition to the ID tag, which every dog should wear even if identified by another method, two other forms of identification have become popular: microchip-

When travel plans can't include your dog, you may need to use a boarding kennel. Be sure that the facilities are immaculately kept and professionally run by caring dog people.

ping and tattooing. In microchipping, a tiny scannable chip is painlessly inserted under the dog's skin. The number is registered to you so that, if your lost dog turns up at a clinic or shelter, the chip can be scanned to retrieve your contact information.

The advantage of the microchip is that it is a permanent form of ID, but there are some factors to consider. Several different companies make microchips, and not all are compatible with the others' scanning devices. It's best to find a company with a universal microchip that can be read by scanners made by other companies as well. It won't do any good to have the dog chipped if the information cannot be retrieved. Also, not every humane society, shelter and clinic is equipped with a scanner, although more and more facilities are equipping themselves. In fact, many shelters microchip dogs that they adopt out to new homes.

Because the microchip is not visible to the eye, the dog must wear a tag that states that he is microchipped so that whoever picks him up will know to have him scanned. He of course also should have a tag with your contact information in case his chip cannot be read. Humane societies and veterinary clinics offer microchipping service, which is usually very affordable.

Though less popular than microchipping, tattooing is

another permanent method of ID for dogs. Most vets perform this service, and there are also clinics that perform dog tattooing. This is also an affordable procedure and one that will not cause much discomfort for the dog. It is best to put the tattoo in a visible area, such as the ear, to deter theft. It is sad to say that there are cases of dogs' being stolen and sold to research laboratories, but such laboratories will not accept tattooed dogs.

To ensure that the tattoo is effective in aiding your dog's return to you, the tattoo number must be registered with a national organization. That way, when someone finds a tattooed dog, a phone call to the registry will quickly match the dog with his owner.

Your Charlie must always have your contact information attached to his everyday collar in addition to any other forms of ID you choose for him.

BASIC TRAINING PRINCIPLES: PUPPY VS. ADULT

There's a big difference between training an adult dog and training a young puppy. With a young puppy, everything is new! At nine or ten weeks of age, he will be experiencing many things, and he has nothing with which to compare these experiences. Up to this point, he has been with his dam and littermates, not one-on-one with people except in his interactions with his breeder and visitors to the litter.

When you first bring the puppy home, he is eager to please you. This means that he accepts doing things your way. During the next couple of months, he will absorb the basis of every-

Perhaps the biggest challenge in training a pup is getting his attention. A tasty tidbit is a sure way to get him to focus and to associate training with fun.

OUR CANINE KIDS

"Everything I learned about parenting, I learned from my dog." How often adults recognize that their parenting skills are mere extensions of the education they acquired while caring for their dogs. Many owners refer to their dogs as their "kids" and treat their canine companions like real members of the family. Surveys indicate that a majority of dog owners talk to their dogs regularly, celebrate their dogs' birthdays and purchase Christmas gifts for their dogs. Another survey shows that dog owners take their dogs to the veterinarian more frequently than they visit their own physicians.

thing he needs to know for the rest of his life. This early age is even referred to as the "sponge" stage. After that, for the next 18 months, it's up to you to reinforce good manners by building on the foundation that you've established. Once your puppy is reliable in basic commands and behavior and has reached the appropriate age, you may gradually introduce him to some of the interesting sports, games and

activities available to pet owners and their dogs.

Raising your puppy is a family affair. Each member of the family must know what rules to set forth for the puppy and how to use the same one-word commands to mean exactly the same thing every time. Even if yours is a large family, one person will soon be considered by the pup to be the leader, the alpha person in his pack, the "boss" who must be obeyed. Often that highly regarded person turns out to be the one who feeds the puppy. Food ranks very high on the puppy's list of important things! That's why your puppy is rewarded with small treats along with verbal praise when he responds to you correctly. As the puppy learns to do what you want him to do, the food rewards are gradually eliminated and only the praise remains. If you were to keep up with the food treats, you could have two problems on your hands—an obese dog and a beggar.

Training begins the minute your English Toy Spaniel puppy steps through the doorway of your home, so don't make the mistake of putting the puppy on the floor and telling him by your actions to "Go for it! Run wild!" Even if this is your first puppy, you must act as if you know what you're doing: be the boss. An uncertain pup may be terrified to move, while a

LEADER OF THE PACK

Canines are pack animals. They live according to pack rules, and every pack has only one leader. Guess what? That's you! To establish your position of authority, lay down the rules and be fair and good-natured in all your dealings with your dog. He will consider young children as his littermates, but the one who trains him, who feeds him, who grooms him, who expects him to come into line, that's his leader. And the one who leads must be obeyed.

It's a big world to a small English Toy puppy! Your pup needs your guidance and training to ensure his safety.

your liking, lucky you! You're off the hook. However, if that dog spent his life up to this point in a kennel, or even in a good home but without any real training, be prepared to tackle the job ahead. A dog three years of age or older with no previous training cannot be blamed for not knowing what he was never taught. While the dog is trying to understand and learn your rules, at the same time he has to unlearn many of his previously self-taught habits and general view of the world.

Working with a professional trainer will speed up your progress with an adopted adult dog. You'll need patience, too. Some new rules may be close to impossible for the dog to accept. After all, he's been successful so far by doing everything his way! (Patience again.) He may agree with your instruction for a few days and then slip back into his old ways, so you must be just as consistent and understanding in your teaching as you would be with a puppy. (More patience needed yet again.) Your dog has to learn to pay attention to your voice, your family, the daily routine, new smells, new sounds and, in some cases, even a new climate.

One of the most important things to find out about a newly adopted adult dog is his reaction to children (yours and others), strangers and your friends, and

bold one will be ready to take you at your word and start plotting to destroy the house! Before you collected your puppy, you decided where his own special place would be, and that's where to put him when you first arrive home. Give him a house tour after he has investigated his area and had a nap and a bathroom "pit stop."

It's worth mentioning here that if you've adopted an adult dog that is completely trained to how he acts upon meeting other dogs. If he was not socialized with dogs as a puppy, this could be a major problem. This does not mean that he's a "bad" dog, a vicious dog or an aggressive dog; rather, it means that he has no idea how to read another dog's body language. There's no way for him to tell whether the other dog is a friend or foe. Survival instinct takes over, telling him to attack first and ask questions later. This definitely calls for professional help and, even then, may not be a behavior that can be corrected 100% reliably (or even at all). If you have a puppy, this is why it is so very important to introduce your young puppy properly to other puppies and "dog-friendly" adult dogs.

HOUSE-TRAINING YOUR ENGLISH TOY SPANIEL

Dogs are tactility-oriented when it comes to house-training. In other words, they respond to the surface on which they are given approval to eliminate. The choice is yours (the dog's version is in parentheses): The lawn (including the neighbors' lawns)? A bare patch of earth under a tree (where people like to sit and relax in the summertime)? Concrete steps or patio (all sidewalks, garages and basement floors)? The curbside (watch out for cars)? A small area of crushed stone in a corner of the yard (mine!)? The latter is the best

KIDS RULE

Children of 10 to 12 year of age are old enough to understand the "be kind to dumb animals" approach and will have fun training their dogs, especially to do tricks. It teaches them to be tolerant, patient and appreciative as well as to accept failure to some extent. Young children can be tyrants, making unreasonable demands of the dog and unable to cope with defeat, blaming it all on the dog. Toddlers need not apply.

choice if you can manage it, because it will remain strictly for the dog's use and is easy to keep clean.

You can start out with paper-training indoors and switch over to an outdoor surface as the puppy matures and gains control over his need to eliminate. For the naysayers, don't worry—this won't mean that the dog will soil on every piece of newspaper lying around the house. You are training him to go outside, remember? Starting out by paper-training often is the only choice for a city dog.

THE RIGHT START

The best advice for a potential dog owner is to start with the very best puppy that money can buy. Don't shop around for a bargain in the newspaper. You're buying a companion, not a used car or a second-hand appliance. The purchase price of the dog represents a very significant part of the investment, but this is indeed a very small sum compared to the expenses of maintaining the dog in good health. If you purchase a well-bred healthy and sound puppy, you will be starting right. An unhealthy puppy can cost you thousands of dollars in unnecessary veterinary expenses and, possibly, a fortune in heartbreak as well.

WHEN YOUR PUPPY'S "GOT TO GO"
Your puppy's need to relieve himself is seemingly non-stop, but signs of improvement will be seen each week. When he first comes home with you, the puppy will have to be taken outside every time he wakes up, about 10–15 minutes after every meal and after every period of play—all day long, from first thing in the morning until his bedtime! That's a total of ten or more trips per day to teach the puppy where it's okay to relieve himself. With that schedule in mind, you can see that house-training a young puppy is not a part-time job. It requires someone to be home all day.

If that seems overwhelming or impossible, do a little planning. For example, plan to pick up your puppy at the start of a vacation period. If you can't get home in the middle of the day, plan to hire a dog-sitter or ask a neighbor to come over to take the pup outside, feed him his lunch and then take him out again about ten or so minutes after he's eaten. Also make arrangements with that or another person to be your "emergency" contact if you have to stay late on the job. Remind yourself—repeatedly—that this hectic schedule improves as the puppy gets older.

HOME WITHIN A HOME

Your English Toy Spaniel puppy needs to be confined to one secure, puppy-proof area when no one is able to watch his every move. Generally the kitchen is the place of choice because the floor is washable. Likewise, it's a busy family area that will accustom the pup to a variety of noises, everything from pots and pans to the telephone, blender and dishwasher. He will also be enchanted by the smell of your cooking (and will never be critical when you burn something). A sturdy exercise pen (also called an "ex-pen," a puppy version of a playpen) within the room of choice can help to confine a young pup. He can see out and has a certain amount of space in which to run about, but he is safe from dangerous things like electrical cords, heating units, trash baskets or open kitchen-supply cabinets. Place the pen where the puppy will not get a blast of heat or air conditioning.

In the pen, you can put a few toys, his bed (which can be his crate if the dimensions of pen and crate are compatible) and a few layers of newspaper in one small corner, just in case. A water bowl can be hung at a convenient height on the side of the ex-pen so it won't become a splashing pool

SMILE WHEN YOU ORDER ME AROUND!

While trainers recommend practicing commands with your dog every day, it's perfectly acceptable to take a "mental health day" off. It's better not to train the dog on days when you're in a sour mood. Your bad attitude or lack of interest will be sensed by your dog, and he will respond accordingly. Studies show that dogs are well tuned in to their humans' emotions. Be conscious of how you use your voice when talking to your dog. Raising your voice or shouting will only erode your dog's trust in you as his trainer and master.

for an innovative puppy. His food dish can go on the floor, next to but not under the water bowl.

Crates are something that pet owners are at last getting used to for their dogs. Wild or domestic canines have always preferred to sleep in den-like safe spots, and that is exactly what the crate provides. How often have you seen adult dogs that choose to sleep under a table or chair even though they have full run of the house? It's the den connection.

In your "happy" voice, use the word "Crate" every time you put the pup into his den. If he's new to a crate, toss in a small biscuit for him to chase the first few times. At night, after he's been outside, he should sleep in his crate. The crate may be kept in his designated area at night or, if you want to be sure to hear those wake-up yips in the morning, put the crate in a corner of your bedroom. However, don't make any response whatsoever to whining or crying. If he's completely ignored, he'll settle down and get to sleep.

Good bedding for a young puppy is an old folded bath towel or an old blanket, something that is easily washable and disposable if necessary ("accidents" will happen!). Never put newspaper in the puppy's crate. Also those old ideas about adding a clock to replace his mother's heartbeat or a hot-water bottle to replace her warmth are just that—old ideas. The clock could drive the puppy nuts, and the hot-water bottle could end up as a very soggy waterbed! An extremely good breeder would have introduced your puppy to the crate by letting two pups sleep together for a couple of nights, followed by

EXTRA! EXTRA!

The headlines read: "Puppy Piddles Here!" Breeders commonly use newspapers to line their whelping pens, so puppies learn to associate newspapers with relieving themselves. Do not use newspapers to line your pup's crate, as this will signal to your puppy that it is OK to urinate in his crate. If you choose to paper-train your puppy, you will layer newspapers on a section of the floor near the door he uses to go outside. You should encourage the puppy to use the papers to relieve himself, and bring him there whenever you see him getting ready to go. Little by little, you will reduce the size of the newspaper-covered area so that the puppy will learn to relieve himself "on the other side of the door."

CANINE DEVELOPMENT SCHEDULE

It is important to understand how and at what age a puppy develops into adulthood. If you are a puppy owner, consult this Canine Development Schedule to determine the stage of development your puppy is currently experiencing. This knowledge will help you as you work with the puppy in the weeks and months ahead.

PERIOD	AGE	CHARACTERISTICS
FIRST TO THIRD	BIRTH TO SEVEN WEEKS	Puppy needs food, sleep and warmth and responds to simple and gentle touching. Needs mother for security and disciplining. Needs littermates for learning and interacting with other dogs. Pup learns to function within a pack and learns pack order of dominance. Begin socializing pup with adults and children for short periods. Pup begins to become aware of his environment.
FOURTH	EIGHT TO TWELVE WEEKS	Brain is fully developed. Pup needs socializing with outside world. Remove from mother and littermates. Needs to change from canine pack to human pack. Human dominance necessary. Fear period occurs between 8 and 12 weeks. Avoid fright and pain.
FIFTH	THIRTEEN TO SIXTEEN WEEKS	Training and formal obedience should begin. Less association with other dogs, more with people, places, situations. Period will pass easily if you remember this is pup's change-to-adolescence time. Be firm and fair. Flight instinct prominent. Permissiveness and over-disciplining can do permanent damage. Praise for good behavior.
JUVENILE	FOUR TO EIGHT MONTHS	Another fear period about seven to eight months of age. It passes quickly, but be cautious of fright and pain. Sexual maturity reached. Dominant traits established. Dog should understand sit, down, come and stay by now.

NOTE: THESE ARE APPROXIMATE TIME FRAMES. ALLOW FOR INDIVIDUAL DIFFERENCES IN PUPPIES.

TIDY BOY

Clean by nature, dogs do not like to soil their dens, which in effect are their crates or sleeping quarters. Unless not feeling well, dogs will not defecate or urinate in their crates. Crate training capitalizes on the dog's natural desire to keep his den clean. Be conscientious about giving the puppy as many opportunities to relieve himself outdoors as possible. Reward the puppy for correct behavior. Praise him and pat him whenever he "goes" in the correct location. Even the tidiest of puppies can have potty accidents, so be patient and dedicate more energy to helping your puppy achieve a clean lifestyle.

several nights alone. How thankful you will be if you found that breeder!

Safe toys in the pup's crate or area will keep him occupied, but monitor their condition closely. Discard any toys that show signs of being chewed to bits. Squeaky parts, bits of stuffing or plastic or any other small pieces can cause intestinal blockage or possibly choking if ingested.

PROGRESSING WITH POTTY-TRAINING

After you've taken your puppy out and he has relieved himself in the area you've selected, he can have some free time with the family as long as there is someone

responsible for watching him. That doesn't mean just someone in the same room who is watching TV or busy on the computer but one person who is doing nothing other than keeping an eye on the pup, playing with him on the floor and helping him understand his position in the pack.

This first taste of freedom will let you begin to set the house rules. If you don't want the dog on the furniture, now is the time to prevent his first attempts to jump up onto the couch. The word to use in this case is "Off," not "Down." "Down" is the word you will use to teach the down position, which is something entirely different.

Most corrections at this stage come in the form of simply distracting the puppy. Instead of telling him "No" for "Don't chew the carpet," distract the chomping puppy with a toy and he'll forget about the carpet.

As you are playing with the pup, do not forget to watch him closely and pay attention to his body language. Whenever you see him begin to circle or sniff, take the puppy outside to relieve himself. If you are paper-training, put him back into his confined area on the newspapers. In either case, praise him as he eliminates while he actually is in the act of relieving himself. Three seconds after he has finished is too late! You'll be praising him for running toward you, picking up a toy or whatever he may be doing at that moment, and that's not what you want to be praising him for. Timing is a vital tool in all dog training. Use it.

Remove soiled newspapers immediately and replace them with clean ones. You may want to take a small piece of soiled paper and place it in the middle of the new clean papers, as the scent will attract him to that spot when it's time to go again. That scent attraction is why it's so important to clean up any messes made in the house by using a product specially made to eliminate the odor of dog urine and droppings. Regular household cleansers won't do the trick. Pet

Training your English Toy puppy ensures that your dog will be a delightful companion and a joy to have in the home.

shops sell the best pet deodorizers. Invest in the largest container you can find.

Scent attraction eventually will lead your pup to his chosen spot outdoors; this is the basis of outdoor training. When you take your puppy outside to relieve himself, use a one-word command such as "Outside" or "Go-potty" (that's one word to the puppy!) as you attach his leash. Then lead him to his spot. Now comes the hard part—hard for you, that is. Just stand there until he urinates and defecates. Move him a few feet in one direction or another if he's just sitting there looking at you, but remember that this is neither playtime nor time for a walk. This is strictly a business trip. Then, as he circles and squats (remember your timing), give him a quiet "Good dog" as praise. If you start to jump for joy, ecstatic over his perform-

DAILY SCHEDULE

How many relief trips does your puppy need per day? A puppy up to the age of 14 weeks will need to go outside about 8 to 12 times per day! You will have to take the pup out any time he starts sniffing around the floor or turning in small circles, as well as after naps, meals, games and lessons or whenever he's released from his crate. Once the puppy is 14 to 22 weeks of age, he will require only 6 to 8 relief trips. At the ages of 22 to 32 weeks, the puppy will require about 5 to 7 trips. Adult dogs typically require 4 relief trips per day, in the morning, afternoon, evening and late at night.

his business and then put back into his area or crate. If you witness an accident in progress, say "No!" in a stern voice and get the pup outdoors immediately. No punishment is needed. You and your puppy are just learning each other's language, and sometimes it's easy to miss a puppy's message. Chalk it up to experience and watch more closely from now on.

KEEPING THE PACK ORDERLY
Discipline is a form of training that brings order to life. For example, military discipline is what allows the soldiers in an army to work as one. Discipline is a form of teaching and, in dogs, is the basis of how the successful pack operates. Each member knows his place in the pack and all respect the leader, or alpha dog. It is essential for your puppy that you establish this type of relationship, with

Training involves teaching the house rules in addition to the basic commands. Will your Charlie be allowed to join you on the sofa? Make a decision and enforce it consistently from puppyhood.

ance, he'll do one of two things: either he will stop mid-stream, as it were, or he'll do it again for you—in the house—and expect you to be just as delighted!

Give him five minutes or so and, if he doesn't go in that time, take him back indoors to his confined area and try again in another ten minutes or immediately if you see him sniffing and circling. By careful observation, you'll soon work out a successful schedule.

Accidents, by the way, are just that—accidents. Clean them up quickly and thoroughly, without comment, after the puppy has been taken outside to finish

KEEP IT SIMPLE—AND FUN
Keep your lessons simple, interesting and user-friendly. Fun breaks help you both. Spend two minutes or ten teaching your puppy, but practice only as long as your dog enjoys what he's doing and is focused on pleasing you. If he's bored or distracted, stop the training session after any correct response (always end on a high note!). After a few minutes of playtime, you can go back to "hitting the books."

you as the alpha, or leader. It is a form of social coexistence that all canines recognize and accept. Discipline, therefore, is never to be confused with punishment. When you teach your puppy how you want him to behave, and he behaves properly and you praise him for it, you are disciplining him with a form of positive reinforcement.

For a dog, rewards come in the form of praise, a smile, a cheerful tone of voice, a few friendly pats or a rub of the ears. Rewards are also small food treats. Obviously, that does not mean bits of regular dog food. Instead, treats are very small bits of special things like cheese or pieces of soft dog treats. The idea is to reward the dog with something very small that he can taste and swallow, providing instant positive reinforcement. If he has to take time to chew the treat, he will have forgotten what he did to earn it by the time he is finished!

Your puppy should never be physically punished. The displeasure shown on your face and in your voice is sufficient to signal to the pup that he has done something wrong. He wants to please everyone higher up on the social ladder, especially his leader, so a scowl and harsh voice will take care of the error. Growling out the word "Shame!" when the pup is caught in the

act of doing something wrong is better than the repetitive "No." Some dogs hear "No" so often that they begin to think it's their name! By the way, do not use the dog's name when you're correcting him. His name is reserved to get his attention for something pleasant about to take place.

There are punishments that have nothing to do with you. For example, your dog may think that chasing cats is one reason for his existence. You can try to stop it as much as you like but without success, because it's such fun for the dog. But one good hissing, spitting swipe of a

Introductions between pets should be supervised so that no trouble arises from surprise meetings. Chances are, these two will grow up together being the best of friends.

Ensure that your English Toy's collar has a proper fit so that it will stay on the dog and be comfortable for him to wear.

cat's claws across the dog's nose will put an end to the game forever. Intervene only when your dog's eyeball is seriously at risk. Cat scratches can cause permanent damage to an innocent but annoying puppy.

PUPPY KINDERGARTEN

COLLAR AND LEASH
Before you begin your English Toy Spaniel puppy's education, he must be used to his collar and leash. Choose a collar for your puppy that is secure but not heavy or bulky. He won't enjoy training if he's uncomfortable. A flat buckle collar is fine for everyday wear and for initial puppy training. For older dogs, there are several types of train-ing collars such as the martin-gale, which is a double loop that tightens slightly around the neck, or the head collar, which is similar to a horse's halter. Do not use a chain choke collar with

TEACHER'S PET
Dogs are individuals, not robots, with many traits basic to their breed. Some, bred to work alone, are independent thinkers; others rely on you to call the shots. If you have enrolled in a training class, your instructor can offer alternative methods of training based on your individual dog's instincts and personality. You may benefit from using a different type of collar or switching to a class with different kinds of dogs.

DON'T STRESS ME OUT

Your dog doesn't have to deal with paying the bills, the daily commute, PTA meetings and the like, but, believe it or not, there's a lot of stress in a dog's world. Stress can be caused by the owner's impatient demeanor and his angry or harsh corrections. If your dog cringes when you reach for his training collar, he's stressed. An older dog is sometimes stressed out when he goes to a new home. No matter what the cause, put off all training until he's over it. If he's going through a fear period—shying away from people, trembling when spoken to, avoiding eye contact or hiding under furniture—wait to resume training. Naturally you'd also postpone your lessons if the dog were sick, and the same goes for you. Show some compassion.

you don't want him to roam away from his area. The shorter leash will also be the one to use when you walk the puppy.

If you've been wise enough to enroll in a puppy kindergarten training class, suggestions will be made as to the best collar and leash for your young puppy. I say "wise" because your puppy will be in a class with puppies in his age range (up to five months old) of all breeds and sizes. It's the perfect way for him to learn the right way (and the wrong way) to interact with other dogs as well as their people. You cannot teach your puppy how to interpret another dog's sign language. For a first-

your English Toy Spaniel. Not only are chain chokes unsuitable for small breeds, they also pull and damage long coats.

A lightweight 6-foot woven cotton or nylon training leash is preferred by most trainers because it is easy to fold up in your hand and comfortable to hold because there is a certain amount of give to it. There are lessons where the dog will start off 6 feet away from you at the end of the leash. The leash used to take the puppy outside to relieve himself is shorter because

Most of all, be positive when approaching the training of your English Toy Spaniel. This is an intelligent and sensitive breed that responds reliably to praise and kindness.

A dog can learn to sit without even knowing it! Initiate the exercise by holding up a treat, and the dog will assume the sit position as he looks up and reaches for it.

EXERCISES FOR A BASIC CANINE EDUCATION

THE SIT EXERCISE

There are several ways to teach the puppy to sit. The first one is to catch him whenever he is about to sit and, as his backside nears the floor, say "Sit, good dog!" That's positive reinforcement and, if your timing is sharp, he will learn that what he's doing at that second is connected to your saying "Sit" and that you think he's clever for doing it!

time puppy owner, these socialization classes are invaluable. For experienced dog owners, they are a real boon to further training.

ATTENTION

You've been using the dog's name since the minute you collected him from the breeder, so you should be able to get his attention by saying his name— with a big smile and in an excited tone of voice. His response will be the puppy equivalent of "Here I am! What are we going to do?" Your immediate response (if you haven't guessed by now) is "Good dog." Rewarding him at the moment he pays attention to you teaches him the proper way to respond when he hears his name.

TIPS FOR TRAINING AND SAFETY

1. Whether on or off leash, practice only in a fenced area.
2. Remove the training collar when the training session is over.
3. Don't try to break up a dogfight.
4. "Come," "Leave it" and "Wait" are safety commands.
5. The dog belongs in a crate or behind a barrier when riding in the car.
6. Don't ignore the dog's first sign of aggression. Aggression only gets worse, so take it seriously.
7. Keep the faces of children and dogs separated.
8. Pay attention to what the dog is chewing.
9. Keep the vet's number near your phone.
10. "Okay" is a useful release command.

Another method is to start with the puppy on his leash in front of you. Show him a treat in the palm of your right hand. Bring your hand up under his nose and, almost in slow motion, move your hand up and back so his nose goes up in the air and his head tilts back as he follows the treat in your hand. At that point, he will have to either sit or fall over, so as his back legs buckle under, say "Sit, good dog," and then give him the treat and lots of praise. You may have to begin with your hand lightly running up his chest, actually lifting his chin up until he sits. Some (usually older) dogs require gentle pressure on their hindquarters with the left hand, in which case the dog should be on your left side. Puppies generally do not appreciate this physical dominance.

Teaching the dog to sit is a very basic exercise and a necessity for a politely behaved dog.

READY, SIT, GO!

On your marks, get set: train! Most professional trainers agree that the sit command is the place to start your dog's formal education. Sitting is a natural posture for most dogs, and they respond to the sit exercise willingly and readily. For every lesson, begin with the sit command so that you start out with a successful exercise; likewise, you should practice the sit command at the end of every lesson as well because you always want to end on a high note.

After a few times, you should be able to show the dog a treat in the open palm of your hand, raise your hand waist-high as you say "Sit" and have him sit. You thereby will have taught him two things at the same time. Both the verbal command and the motion of the hand are signals for the sit. Your puppy is watching you almost more than he is listening to you, so what you do is just as important as what you say.

Don't save any of these drills only for training sessions. Use them as much as possible at odd times during a normal day. The

dog should always sit before being given his food dish. He should sit to let you go through a doorway first, when the doorbell rings or when you stop to speak to someone on the street.

THE DOWN EXERCISE

Before beginning to teach the down command, you must consider how the dog feels about this exercise. To him, "down" is a submissive position. Being flat on the floor with you standing over him is not his idea of fun. It's up to you to let him know that, while it may not be fun, the reward of your approval is worth his effort.

Start with the puppy on your left side in a sit position. Hold the leash right above his collar in your left hand. Have an extra-special treat, such as a small piece of cooked chicken or hot dog, in your right hand. Place it at the end of the pup's nose and steadily move your hand down and forward along the ground. Hold the leash to prevent a sudden lunge for the food. As the puppy goes into the down position, say "Down" very gently.

The difficulty with this exercise is twofold: it's both the submissive aspect and the fact that most people say the word "Down" as if they were drill sergeants in charge of recruits! So issue the command sweetly, give him the treat and have the pup maintain the down position for several seconds. If he tries to get up immediately, place your hands on his shoulders and press down gently, giving him a very quiet "Good dog." As you progress with this lesson, increase the "down time" until he will hold it until you say "Okay" (his cue for release). Practice this one in the house at various times throughout the day.

By increasing the length of time during which the dog must maintain the down position, you'll find many uses for it. For example, he can lie at your feet in the vet's office or anywhere that both of you have to wait, when you are on the phone, while the family is eating and so forth. If you progress to training for competitive obedience, he'll already be all set for the exercise called the "long down."

Teaching the down exercise may require a little extra coaxing and reassurance— and a food reward always helps!

THE STAY EXERCISE

You can teach your English Toy Spaniel to stay in the sit, down and stand positions. To teach the sit/stay, have the dog sit on your left side. Hold the leash at waist level in your left hand, and let the dog know that you have a treat in your closed right hand. Step forward on your right foot as you say "Stay." Immediately turn and stand directly in front of the dog, keeping your right hand up high so he'll keep his eye on the treat hand and maintain the sit posi-tion for a count of five. Return to your original position and offer the reward.

Increase the length of the sit/stay each time until the dog can hold it for at least 30 seconds without moving. After about a week of success, move out on your right foot and take two steps before turning to face the dog. Give the "Stay" hand signal (left palm back toward the dog's head) as you leave. He gets the treat when you return and he holds the sit/stay. Increase the distance

The intelligent and alert English Toy Spaniel makes a bright and attentive student.

that you walk away from him before turning until you reach the length of your training leash. But don't rush it! Go back to the beginning if he moves before he should. No matter what the lesson, never be upset by having to back up for a few days. The repetition and practice are what will make your dog reliable in these commands. It won't do any good to move on to something more difficult if the command is not mastered at the easier levels. Above all, even if you do get frustrated, never let your puppy know! Always keep a positive, upbeat attitude during training, which will transmit to your dog for positive results.

The down/stay is taught in the same way once the dog is completely reliable and steady with the down command. Again, don't rush it. With the dog in the down position on your left side, step out on your right foot as you say "Stay." Return by walking around in back of the dog and into your original position. While you are training, it's okay to murmur something like "Hold on" to encourage him to stay put. When the dog will stay without moving when you are at a distance of 3 or 4 feet, begin to increase the length of time before you return. Be sure he holds the down on your return until you say "Okay." At that point, he gets his treat—just so he'll remember for next time that it's not over until it's over.

THE COME EXERCISE

No command is more important to the safety of your English Toy Spaniel than "Come." It is what you should say every single time

I WILL FOLLOW YOU

Obedience isn't just a classroom activity. In your home you have many great opportunities to teach your dog polite manners. Allowing your pet on the bed or furniture elevates him to your level, which is not a good idea (the word is "Off!"). Use the "umbilical cord" method, keeping your dog on lead so he has to go with you wherever you go. You sit, he sits. You walk, he heels. You stop, he sit/stays. Everywhere you go, he's with you, but you go first!

you see the puppy running toward you: "Ringo, come! Good dog." During playtime, run a few feet away from the puppy and turn and tell him to "Come" as he is already running to you. You can go so far as to teach your puppy two things at once if you squat down and hold out your arms. As the pup gets close to you and you're saying "Good dog," bring your right arm in about waist high. Now he's also learning the hand signal, an excellent device should you be on the phone when you need to get him to come to you! You'll also both be one step ahead when you enter obedience classes.

When the puppy responds to your well-timed "Come," try it with the puppy on the training leash. This time, catch him off guard, while he's sniffing a leaf or watching a bird: "Ringo, come!" You may have to pause for a split second after his name to be sure you have his attention. If the puppy shows any sign of confusion, give the leash a mild jerk and take a couple of steps backward. Do not repeat the command. In this case, you should say "Good come" as he reaches you.

That's the number-one rule of training. Each command word is given just once. Anything more is nagging. You'll also notice that all commands are one word only. Even when they are actually two words, you say them as one.

COME AND GET IT!

The come command is your dog's safety signal. Until he is 99% perfect in responding, don't use the come command if you cannot enforce it. Practice on leash with treats or squeakers, or whenever the dog is running to you. Never call him to come to you if he is to be corrected for a misdemeanor. Reward the dog with a treat and happy praise whenever he comes to you.

Never call the dog to come to you—with or without his name—if you are angry or intend to correct him for some misbehavior. When correcting the pup, you go to him. Your dog must always connect "Come" with something pleasant and with your approval; then you can rely on his response.

Puppies, like children, have notoriously short attention spans, so don't overdo it with any of the

be in control. Besides, it looks terrible to have your dog straining at the leash, and it's not much fun either. At first, your young puppy will probably follow you everywhere, but that's his natural instinct, not your control over the situation. However, any time he does follow you, you can say "Heel" and be ahead of the game, as he will learn to associate this command with the action of following you before you even begin teaching him to heel.

There is a very precise, almost military, procedure for teaching your dog to heel. As

Though an English Toy won't be pulling many people down the street, it still is no fun to walk a dog who doesn't behave on leash. training. Keep each lesson short. Break it up with a quick run around the yard or a ball toss, repeat the lesson and quit as soon as the pup gets it right. That way, you will always end with a "Good dog."

Life isn't perfect and neither are puppies. A time will come, often around ten months of age, when he'll become "selectively deaf" or choose to "forget" his name. He may respond by wagging his tail (and even seeming to smile at you) with a look that says "Make me!" Laugh, throw his favorite toy and skip the lesson you had planned. Pups will be pups!

THE HEEL EXERCISE

The second most important command to teach, after the come, is the heel. When you are walking your growing puppy, you need to

FEAR AGGRESSION

Of the several types of aggression, the one brought on by fear is the most difficult for people to comprehend and to deal with. Aggression to protect food, or any object the dog perceives as his, is more easily understood. Fear aggression is quite different. The dog shows fear, generally for no apparent reason. He backs off, cowers or hides under the bed. If he's on lead, he will hide behind your leg and lash out unexpectedly. No matter how you approach him, he will bite. A fear-biter attacks with great speed and instantly retreats. Don't shout at him or go near him. Don't coddle, sympathize or try to protect him. To him, that's a reward. As with other forms of aggression, get professional help.

with all other obedience training, begin with the dog on your left side. He will be in a very nice sit and you will have the training leash across your chest. Hold the loop and folded leash in your right hand. Pick up the slack leash above the dog in your left hand and hold it loosely at your side. Step out on your left foot as you say "Heel." If the puppy does not move, give a gentle tug or pat your left leg to get him started. If he surges ahead of you, stop and pull him back gently until he is at your side. Tell him to sit and begin again.

Once your Charlie is heel-trained, your daily walks will be enjoyable outings for both of you.

TIME TO PLAY!

Playtime can happen both indoors and out. A young puppy is growing so rapidly that he needs sleep more than he needs a lot of physical exercise. Puppies get sufficient exercise on their own just through normal puppy activity. Monitor play with young children so you can remove the puppy when he's had enough, or calm the kids if they get too rowdy. Almost all puppies love to chase after a toy you've thrown, and you can turn your games into educational activities. Every time your puppy brings the toy back to you, say "Give it" (or "Drop it") followed by "Good dog" and throwing it again. If he's reluctant to give it to you, offer a small treat so that he drops the toy as he takes the treat. He will soon get the idea.

Walk a few steps and stop while the puppy is correctly beside you. Tell him to sit and give mild verbal praise. (More enthusiastic praise will encourage him to think the lesson is over.) Repeat the lesson, increasing the number of steps you take only as long as the dog is heeling nicely beside you. When you end the lesson, have him hold the sit, then give him the "Okay" to let him know that this is the end of the lesson. Praise him so that he knows he did a good job.

The cure for excessive pulling (a common problem) is to stop when the dog is no more than 2 or 3 feet ahead of you. Guide him back into position and begin again. With a really determined puller, try switching to a head collar. When used properly, this will turn the pup's head toward you so you can bring him back easily to the heel position. Give quiet, reassuring praise every time the leash goes slack and he's staying with you.

Staying and heeling can take a lot out of a dog, so provide playtime and free-running exercise to shake off the stress when the lessons are over. You don't want him to associate training with all work and no fun.

TAPERING OFF TIDBITS
Your dog has been watching you—and the hand that treats—throughout all of his lessons, and now it's time to break the treat habit. Begin by giving him treats at the end of each lesson only. Then start to give a treat after the end of only

---

LET'S GO!
Many people use "Let's go" instead of "Heel" when teaching their dogs to behave on lead. It sounds more like fun! When beginning to teach the heel, whatever command you use, always step off on your left foot. That's the one next to the dog, who is on your left side, in case you've forgotten. Keep a loose leash. When the dog pulls ahead, stop, bring him back and begin again. Use treats to guide him around turns.

---

some of the lessons. At the end of every lesson, as well as during the lessons, be consistent with the praise. Your pup now doesn't know whether he'll get a treat or not, but he should keep performing well just in case! Finally, you will stop giving treat rewards entirely. Save them for something brand-new that you want to teach him. Keep up the praise and you'll always have a "good dog."

OBEDIENCE CLASSES
The advantages of an obedience class are that your dog will have to learn amid the distractions of other people and dogs and that your mistakes will be quickly corrected by the trainer. Teaching your dog along with a qualified instructor and other handlers who may have more dog experience than you is another plus of the class environment. The instructor and other handlers can help you to find the most efficient way of teaching your dog a command or exercise. It's often easier to learn by other people's mistakes than your own. You will also learn all of the requirements for competitive obedience trials, in which you can earn titles and go on to advanced jumping and retrieving exercises, which are fun for many dogs. Obedience classes build the foundation needed for many other canine activities (in which we humans are allowed to participate, too!).

NO MORE TREATS!

When your dog is responding promptly and correctly to commands, it's time to eliminate treats. Begin by alternating a treat reward with a verbal-praise-only reward. Gradually eliminate all treats while increasing the frequency of praise. Overlook pleading eyes and expectant expressions, but if he's still watching your treat hand, you're on your way to using hand signals.

TRAINING FOR OTHER ACTIVITIES

Once your dog has basic obedience under his collar and is 12 months of age, you can enter the world of agility training. Dogs think agility is pure fun, like being turned loose in an amusement park full of obstacles! In addition to agility, there are other types of competitive events such as rally obedience and tracking, which is open to all "nosey" dogs (which would include all dogs!). For those who like to volunteer, there is the wonderful feeling of owning a therapy dog and visiting hospices, nursing homes and veterans' homes to bring smiles, comfort and companionship to those who live there.

Around the house, your English Toy Spaniel can be taught to do some simple chores. You might teach him to carry small household items or even to fetch

things for you. The kids can teach the dog all kinds of tricks, from playing hide-and-seek to balancing a biscuit on his nose. A family dog is what rounds out the family. Everything he does, including sitting in your lap and gazing lovingly at you, represents the bonus of owning a dog.

A well-socialized, well-trained English Toy will act appropriately when the two of you are out and about.

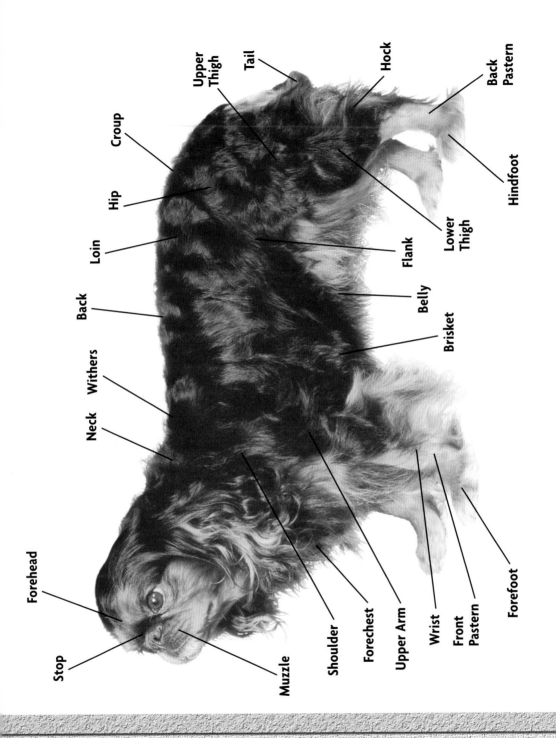

Forehead

Stop

Muzzle

Neck

Withers

Back

Loin

Hip

Croup

Upper Thigh

Tail

Hock

Back Pastern

Hindfoot

Lower Thigh

Flank

Belly

Brisket

Shoulder

Forechest

Upper Arm

Wrist

Front Pastern

Forefoot

PHYSICAL STRUCTURE OF THE ENGLISH TOY SPANIEL

ENGLISH TOY SPANIEL

By Lowell Ackerman DVM, DACVD

HEALTHCARE FOR A LIFETIME

When you own a dog, you become his healthcare advocate over his entire lifespan, as well as being the one to shoulder the financial burden of such care. Accordingly, it is worthwhile to focus on prevention rather than treatment, as you and your pet will both be happier.

Of course, the best place to have begun your program of preventive healthcare is with the initial purchase or adoption of your dog. There is no way of guaranteeing that your new furry friend is free of medical problems, but there are some things you can do to improve your odds. You certainly should have done adequate research into the English Toy Spaniel and have selected your puppy carefully rather than buying on impulse. Health issues aside, a large number of pet abandonment and relinquishment cases arise from a mismatch between pet needs and owner expectations. This is entirely preventable with appropriate planning and finding a good breeder.

Regarding healthcare issues specifically, it is very difficult to make blanket statements about where to acquire a problem-free pet, but, again, a reputable breeder is your best bet. In an ideal situation you have the opportunity to see both parents, get references from other owners of the breeder's pups and see genetic-testing documentation for several generations of the litter's ancestors. At the very least, you must thoroughly investigate the English Toy Spaniel and the problems inherent in that breed, as well as the genetic testing available to screen for those problems. Genetic testing offers some important benefits, but this testing is available for only a few disorders in a relatively small number of breeds and is not available for some of the most common genetic diseases, such as hip dysplasia, cataracts, epilepsy, cardiomyopathy, etc. This area of research is indeed exciting and increasingly important, and advances will continue to be made each year. In fact, recent research has shown that there is an equivalent dog gene for 75% of known human genes, so research done in either species is likely to benefit the other.

1. Trachea
2. Lungs
3. Heart
4. Liver
5. Stomach
6. Intestines
7. Urinary Bladder

INTERNAL ORGANS OF THE ENGLISH TOY SPANIEL

We've also discussed that evaluating the behavioral nature of your English Toy Spaniel and that of his immediate family members is an important part of the selection process that cannot be overemphasized. It is sometimes difficult to evaluate temperament in puppies because certain behavioral tendencies, such as some forms of aggression, may not be immediately evident. More dogs are euthanized each year for behavioral reasons than for all medical conditions combined, so it is critical to take temperament issues seriously. Start with a well-balanced, friendly companion and put the time and effort into proper socialization, and you will both be rewarded with a valued relationship for the life of the dog.

Assuming that you have started off with a pup from healthy, sound stock, you then become responsible for helping your veterinarian keep your pet healthy. Some crucial things happen before you even bring your puppy home. Parasite control typically begins at two weeks of age, and vaccinations typically begin at six to eight weeks of age. A pre-pubertal evaluation is typically scheduled for about six months of age. At this time, a dental evaluation is done (since the adult teeth are now in), heartworm prevention is started and neutering or spaying is most commonly done.

It is critical to commence regular dental care at home if you have not already done so. It may not sound very important, but most dogs have active periodontal disease by four years of age if they don't have their teeth cleaned regularly at home, not just at their veterinary exams. Dental problems lead to more than just bad "doggy breath." Gum disease can have very serious medical consequences. If you start brushing your dog's teeth and using antiseptic rinses from a young age, your dog will be accustomed to it and will not resist. The results will be healthy dentition, which your pet will need to enjoy a long, healthy life.

Most dogs are considered adults at a year of age, although some larger breeds still have some filling out to do up to about two or so years old. Even individual dogs within each breed have different healthcare requirements, so work with your veterinarian to determine what will be needed and what your role should be. This doctor-client relationship is important, because as vaccination guidelines change, there may not be an annual "vaccine visit" scheduled. You must make sure that you see your veterinarian at least annually, even if no vaccines are due, because this is the best opportunity to coordinate healthcare activities and to make sure that

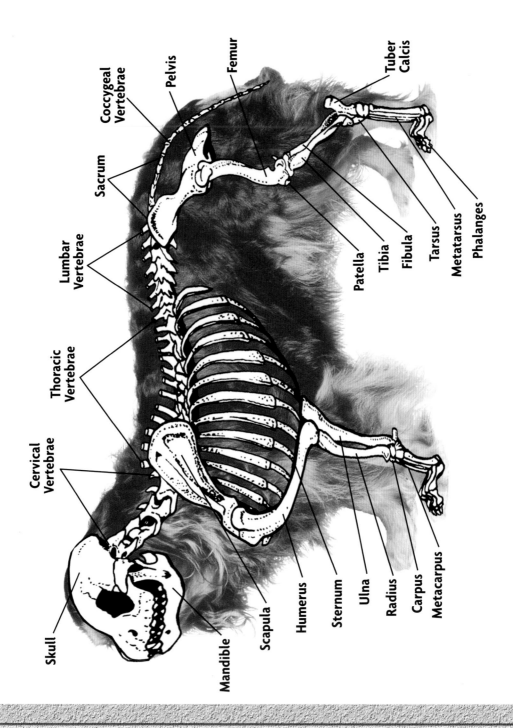

Coccygeal Vertebrae

Pelvis

Femur

Tuber Calcis

Sacrum

Phalanges

Metatarsus

Tarsus

Fibula

Tibia

Patella

Lumbar Vertebrae

Thoracic Vertebrae

Cervical Vertebrae

Skull

Mandible

Scapula

Humerus

Sternum

Ulna

Radius

Carpus

Metacarpus

SKELETAL STRUCTURE OF THE ENGLISH TOY SPANIEL

no medical issues creep by unaddressed.

When your English Toy Spaniel reaches three-quarters of his anticipated lifespan, he is considered a "senior" and likely requires some special care. In general, if you've been taking great care of your canine companion throughout his formative and adult years, the transition to senior status should be a smooth one. Age is not a disease, and as long as everything is functioning as it should, there is no reason why most of late adulthood should not be rewarding for both you and your pet. This is especially true if you have tended to the details, such as regular veterinary visits, proper dental care, excellent nutrition and management of bone and joint issues.

At this stage in your English Toy Spaniel's life, your veterinarian may want to schedule visits twice yearly, instead of once, to run some laboratory screenings, electrocardiograms and the like and to change the diet to something more digestible. Catching problems early is the best way to manage them effectively. Treating the early stages of heart disease is so much easier than trying to intervene when there is more significant damage to the heart muscle. Similarly, managing the beginning of kidney problems is fairly routine if there is no significant kidney damage. Other problems, like cognitive dysfunction (similar to senility and Alzheimer's disease), cancer, diabetes and arthritis, are more common in older dogs, but all can be treated to help the dog live as

PROBLEM: AND THAT STARTS WITH "P"

Urinary tract problems more commonly affect female dogs, especially those who have been spayed. The first sign that a urinary tract problem exists usually is a strong odor from the urine or an unusual color. Blood in the urine, known as hematuria, is another sign of an infection, related to cystitis, a bladder infection, bladder cancer or a blood-clotting disorder. Urinary tract problems can also be signaled by the dog's straining while urinating, experiencing pain during urination and genital discharge as well as excessive water intake and urination.

Excessive drinking, in and of itself, does not indicate a urinary tract problem. A dog who is drinking more than normal may have a kidney or liver problem, a hormonal disorder or diabetes mellitus. Behaviorists report a disorder known as psychogenic polydipsia, which manifests itself in excessive drinking and urination. If you notice your dog drinking much more than normal, take him to the vet.

many happy, comfortable years as possible. Just as in people,

medical management is more effective (and less expensive) when you catch things early.

SELECTING A VETERINARIAN
There is probably no more important decision that you will make regarding your pet's healthcare than the selection of his doctor. Your pet's veterinarian will be a pediatrician, family-practice physician and gerontologist, depending on the dog's life stage, and will be the individual who makes recommendations regarding issues such as when specialists need to be consulted, when diagnostic testing and/or therapeutic intervention is needed and when you will need to seek outside emergency and critical-care services. Your vet will act as your advocate and liaison throughout these processes.

Everyone has his own idea about what to look for in a vet, an individual who will play a big role in his dog's (and, of course, his own) life for many years to come. For some, it is the compassionate caregiver with whom they hope to develop a professional relationship to span the lives of their dogs and even their future pets. For others, they are seeking a clinician with keen diagnostic and therapeutic insight who can deliver state-of-the-art healthcare. Still others need a veterinary facility that is open evenings and weekends, is in close proximity or provides mobile veterinary services to accommodate their schedules; these people may not much mind that their dogs might see different veterinarians on each visit. Just as we have different reasons for selecting our own healthcare professionals (e.g., covered by insurance plan, expert in field, convenient location, etc.), we should not expect that there is a one-size-fits-all recommendation for selecting a veterinarian and veterinary practice. The best advice is to be honest in your assessment of what you expect from a veterinary practice and to conscientiously research the options in your area. You will quickly appreciate that not all veterinary practices are the same, and you will be happiest with one that truly meets your needs.

There is another point to be considered in the selection of veterinary services. Not that long ago, a single veterinarian would attempt to manage all medical and surgical issues as they arose. That was often problematic, because veterinarians are trained in many species and many diseases, and it was just impossible for general veterinary practitioners to be experts in every species, every breed, every field and every ailment. However, just as in the human healthcare fields, specialization has allowed general practitioners to concentrate on primary healthcare delivery, especially

wellness and the prevention of infectious diseases, and to utilize a network of specialists to assist in the management of conditions that require specific expertise and experience. Thus there are now many types of veterinary specialists, including dermatologists, cardiologists, ophthalmologists, surgeons, internists, oncologists, neurologists, behaviorists, criticalists and others to help primary-care veterinarians deal with complicated medical challenges. In most cases, specialists see cases referred by primary-care veterinarians, make diagnoses and set up management plans. From there, the animals' ongoing care is returned to their primary-care veterinarians. This important team approach to your pet's medical-care needs has provided opportunities for advanced care and an unparalleled level of quality to be delivered.

With all of the opportunities for your English Toy Spaniel to receive high-quality veterinary medical care, there is another topic that needs to be addressed at the same time—cost. It's been said that you can have excellent healthcare or inexpensive healthcare, but never both; this is as true in veterinary medicine as it is in human medicine. While veterinary costs are a fraction of what the same services cost in the human healthcare arena, it is still difficult to deal with unantici-

Vaccinations are given to your Charlie as a puppy. Booster shots, when necessary, are one of the things you can expect at his annual veterinary check-ups throughout his life.

and that you are actually buying an indemnity insurance plan from an insurance company that is regulated by your state or province. Many insurance policy look-alikes are actually discount clubs that are redeemable only at specific locations and for specific services. An indemnity plan covers your pet at almost all veterinary, specialty and emergency practices and is an excellent way to manage your pet's ongoing healthcare needs.

pated medical costs, especially since they can easily creep into hundreds or even thousands of dollars if specialists or emergency services become involved. However, there are ways of managing these risks. The easiest is to buy pet health insurance and realize that its foremost purpose is not to cover routine healthcare visits but rather to serve as an umbrella for those rainy days when your pet needs medical care and you don't want to worry about whether or not you can afford that care.

Pet insurance policies are very cost-effective (and very inexpensive by human health-insurance standards), but make sure that you buy the policy long before you intend to use it (preferably starting in puppy-hood, because coverage will exclude pre-existing conditions)

TAKING YOUR DOG'S TEMPERATURE

It is important to know how to take your dog's temperature at times when you think he may be ill. It's not the most enjoyable task, but it can be done without too much difficulty. It's easier with a helper, preferably someone with whom the dog is friendly, so that one of you can hold the dog while the other inserts the thermometer.

Before inserting the thermometer, coat the end with petroleum jelly. Insert the thermometer slowly and gently into the dog's rectum about one inch. Wait for the reading, about two minutes. Be sure to remove the thermometer carefully and clean it thoroughly after each use.

A dog's normal body temperature is between 100.5 and 102.5 degrees F. Immediate veterinary attention is required if the dog's temperature is below 99 or above 104 degrees F.

VACCINATIONS AND INFECTIOUS DISEASES

There has never been an easier time to prevent a variety of infectious diseases in your dog, but the advances we've made in veterinary medicine come with a price—choice. Now while it may seem that choice is a good thing (and it is), it has never been more difficult for the pet owner (or the veterinarian) to make an informed decision about the best way to protect pets through vaccination.

Years ago, it was just accepted that puppies got a starter series of vaccinations and then annual "boosters" throughout their lives to keep them protected. As more and more vaccines became available, consumers wanted the convenience of having all of that protection in a single injection. The result was "multivalent" vaccines that crammed a lot of protection into a single syringe. The manufacturers' recommendations were to give the vaccines annually, and this was a simple enough protocol to follow. However, as veterinary medicine has become more sophisticated and we have started looking more at healthcare quandaries rather than convenience, it became necessary to reevaluate the situation and deal with some tough questions. It is important to realize that whether or not to use a particular vaccine depends on the risk of contracting the disease against

---

BEWARE THE SPIDER

Should you worry about having a spider spinning her mucilaginous web over your dog? Like other venomous critters, spiders can bite dogs and cause severe reactions. The most deleterious eight-leggers are the black and red widow spiders, brown recluse and common brown spiders, whose bites can cause local pain, cramping, spasms and restlessness. These signals tell owners there is a problem, as the bites themselves can be difficult to locate under your dog's coat. Another vicious arachnid is the bark scorpion, whose bite can cause excessive drooling, tearing, urination and defecation. Often spider and scorpion bites are misdiagnosed because vets don't recognize the signs and owners didn't witness the escape of the avenging arachnid.

---

which it protects, the severity of the disease if it is contracted, the duration of immunity provided by the vaccine, the safety of the product and the needs of the individual animal. In a very general sense, rabies, distemper, hepatitis and parvovirus are considered core vaccine needs, while parainfluenza, *Bordetella bronchiseptica*, leptospirosis, coronavirus and borreliosis (Lyme disease) are considered non-core needs and best reserved for animals that demonstrate reasonable risk of contracting the diseases.

NEUTERING/SPAYING

Sterilization procedures (neutering for males/spaying for females) are meant to accomplish several purposes. While the underlying premise is to address the risk of pet overpopulation, there are some medical and behavioral benefits to the surgeries as well. For females, spaying prior to the first estrus (heat cycle) leads to a marked reduction in the risk of mammary cancer and other serious female health problems. There also will be no manifesta-tions of "heat" to attract male dogs and no bleeding in the house. For males, there is prevention of testicular cancer and a reduction in the risk of prostate problems. In both sexes there may be some limited reduction in aggressive behaviors toward other dogs, and some diminishing of urine marking, roaming and mounting.

While neutering and spaying do indeed prevent animals from contributing to pet overpopulation, even no-cost and low-cost neutering options have not eliminated the problem. Perhaps one of the main reasons for this is that individuals that intentionally breed their dogs and those that allow their animals to run at large are the main causes of unwanted offspring. Also, animals in shelters are often there because they were abandoned or relinquished, not because they came from unplanned matings. Neutering/spaying is important, but it should be considered in the context of the real causes of animals' ending up in shelters and eventually being euthanized.

One of the important considerations regarding neutering is that it is a surgical procedure. This sometimes gets lost in discussions of low-cost procedures and commoditization of the process. In females, spaying is specifically referred to as an ovariohysterectomy. In this proce-

---

SPAY'S THE WAY

Although spaying a female dog qualifies as major surgery—an ovariohysterectomy, in fact—this procedure is regarded as routine when performed by a qualified veterinarian on a healthy dog. The advantages to spaying a bitch are many and great. Spayed dogs do not develop uterine cancer or any life-threatening diseases of the genitals. Likewise, spayed dogs are at a significantly reduced risk of breast cancer. Bitches (and owners) are relieved of the demands of heat cycles. A spayed bitch will not leave bloody stains on your furniture during estrus, and you will not have to contend with single-minded macho males trying to climb your fence in order to seduce her. The spayed bitch's coat will not show the ill effects of her estrogen level's climbing such as a dull, lackluster outer coat or patches of hairlessness.

dure, a midline incision is made in the abdomen and the entire uterus and both ovaries are surgically removed. While this is a major invasive surgical procedure, it usually has few complications, because it is typically performed on healthy young animals. However, it is major surgery, as any woman who has had a hysterectomy will attest.

In males, neutering has traditionally referred to castration, which involves the surgical removal of both testicles. While still a significant piece of surgery, there is not the abdominal exposure that is required in the female surgery. In addition, there is now a chemical sterilization option, in which a solution is injected into each testicle, leading to atrophy of the sperm-producing cells. This can typically be done under sedation rather than full anesthesia. This is a relatively new approach, and there are no long-term clinical studies yet available.

Neutering/spaying is typically done around six months of age at most veterinary hospitals, although techniques have been pioneered to perform the procedures in animals as young as eight weeks of age. In general, the surgeries on the very young animals are done for the specific reason of sterilizing them before they go to their new homes. This is done in some shelter hospitals for assurance that the animals

DENTAL WARNING SIGNS
A veterinary dental exam is necessary if you notice one or any combination of the following in your dog:
- Broken, loose or missing teeth
- Loss of appetite (which could be due to mouth pain or illness caused by infection)
- Gum abnormalities, including redness, swelling and bleeding
- Drooling, with or without blood
- Yellowing of the teeth or gumline, indicating tartar
- Bad breath

will definitely not produce any pups. Otherwise, these organizations need to rely on owners to comply with their wishes to have the animals "altered" at a later date, something that does not always happen.

There are some exciting immunocontraceptive "vaccines" currently under development, and there may be a time when contraception in pets will not require surgical procedures. We anxiously await these developments.

S. E. M. by Dr. Dennis Kunkel, University of Hawaii.

A scanning electron micrograph of a dog flea, **Ctenocephalides canis,** *on dog hair.*

warmth of the animals' bodies, movement and exhaled carbon dioxide. However, when they first emerge from their cocoons, they orient towards light; thus when an animal passes between a flea and the light source, casting a shadow, the flea pounces and starts to feed. If the animal turns out to be a dog or cat, the reproductive cycle continues. If the flea lands on another type of animal, including a

EXTERNAL PARASITES

FLEAS

Fleas have been around for millions of years and, while we have better tools now for controlling them than at any time in the past, there still is little chance that they will end up on an endangered species list. Actually, they are very well adapted to living on our pets, and they continue to adapt as we make advances.

The female flea can consume 15 times her weight in blood during active reproduction and can lay as many as 40 eggs a day. These eggs are very resistant to the effects of insecticides. They hatch into larvae, which then mature and spin cocoons. The immature fleas reside in this pupal stage until the time is right for feeding. This pupal stage is also very resistant to the effects of insecticides, and pupae can last in the environment without feeding for many months. Newly emergent fleas are attracted to animals by the

FLEA PREVENTION FOR YOUR DOG

- Discuss with your veterinarian the safest product to protect your dog, likely in the form of a monthly tablet or a liquid preparation placed on the back of the dog's neck.
- For dogs suffering from flea-bite dermatitis, a shampoo or topical insecticide treatment is required.
- Your lawn and property should be sprayed with an insecticide designed to kill fleas and ticks that lurk outdoors.
- Using a flea comb, check the dog's coat regularly for any signs of parasites.
- Practice good housekeeping. Vacuum floors, carpets and furniture regularly, especially in the areas that the dog frequents, and wash the dog's bedding weekly.
- Follow up house-cleaning with carpet shampoos and sprays to rid the house of fleas at all stages of development. Insect growth regulators are the safest option.

person, the flea will bite but will then look for a more appropriate host. An emerging adult flea can survive without feeding for up to 12 months but, once it tastes blood, it can survive off its host for only 3 to 4 days.

It was once thought that fleas spend most of their lives in the environment, but we now know that fleas won't willingly jump off a dog unless leaping to another dog or when physically removed by brushing, bathing or other manipulation. Flea eggs, on the other hand, are shiny and smooth, and they roll off the animal and into the environment. The eggs, larvae and pupae then exist in the environment, but once the adult finds a susceptible animal, it's home sweet home until the flea is forced to seek refuge elsewhere.

Since adult fleas live on the animal and immature forms survive in the environment, a successful treatment plan must address all stages of the flea life cycle. There are now several safe and effective flea-control products that can be applied on a monthly basis. These include fipronil, imidacloprid, selamectin and permethrin (found in several formulations). Most of these products have significant flea-killing rates within 24 hours. However, none of them will control the immature forms in the environment. To accomplish this, there are a variety of insect growth regulators that can be sprayed into the envi-

THE FLEA'S LIFE CYCLE

What came first, the flea or the egg? This age-old mystery is more difficult to comprehend than the actual cycle of the flea. Fleas usually live only about four months. A female can lay 2,000 eggs in her lifetime.

PHOTO BY CAROLINA BIOLOGICAL SUPPLY CO.

Egg

After ten days of rolling around your carpet or under your furniture, the eggs hatch into larvae, which feed on various and sundry debris. In days or

Larva

PHOTO BY CAROLINA BIOLOGICAL SUPPLY CO.

months, depending on the climate, the larvae spin cocoons and develop into the pupal or nymph stage, which quickly develop into fleas.

Pupa

These immature fleas must locate a host within 10 to 14 days or they will die. Only about 1% of the flea population exist as adult fleas, while the other 99% exist as eggs, larvae or pupae.

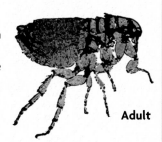

Adult

ronment (e.g., pyriproxyfen, methoprene, fenoxycarb) as well as insect development inhibitors such as lufenuron that can be administered. These compounds have no effect on adult fleas, but they stop immature forms from developing into adults. In years gone by, we relied heavily on toxic insecticides (such as organophosphates, organochlorines and carbamates) to manage the flea problem, but today's options are not only much safer to use on our pets but also safer for the environment.

TICKS

Ticks are members of the spider class (arachnids) and are blood-sucking parasites capable of transmitting a variety of diseases, including Lyme disease, ehrlichiosis, babesiosis and Rocky Mountain spotted fever. It's easy to see ticks on your own skin, but it is more of a challenge when your furry companion is affected. Whenever you happen to be planning a stroll in a tick-infested area (especially forests, grassy or wooded areas or parks) be prepared to do a thorough inspection of your dog afterward to search for ticks. Ticks can be tricky,

> **TICK CONTROL**
> Removal of underbrush and leaf litter and the thinning of trees in areas where tick control is desired are recommended. These actions remove the cover and food sources for small animals that serve as hosts for ticks. With continued mowing of grasses in these areas, the probability of ticks' surviving is further reduced. A variety of insecticide ingredients (e.g., resmethrin, carbaryl, permethrin, chlorpyrifos, dioxathion and allethrin) are registered for tick control around the home.

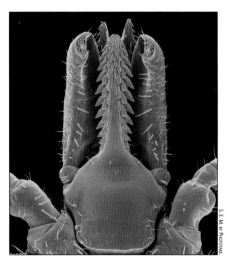

A scanning electron micrograph of the head of a female deer tick, *Ixodes dammini*, a parasitic tick that carries Lyme disease.

S. E. M. BY PHOTOTAKE.

so make sure you spend time looking in the ears, between the toes and everywhere else where a tick might hide. Ticks need to be attached for 24–72 hours before they transmit most of the diseases that they carry, so you do have a window of opportunity for some preventive intervention.

Female ticks live to eat and breed. They can lay between 4,000 and 5,000 eggs and they die soon after. Males, on the other hand, live only to mate with the females and continue the process as long as they are able. Most ticks live on multiple hosts before parasitizing dogs. The immature forms typically reside on grass and shrubs, waiting for susceptible animals to walk by. The larvae and nymph stages typically feed on wildlife.

If only a few ticks are present on a dog, they can be plucked out, but it is important to remove the

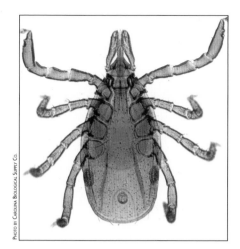

PHOTO BY CAROLINA BIOLOGICAL SUPPLY CO.

Skin diseases caused by mites are referred to as "mange," and there are many different forms seen in dogs. These forms are very different from one another, each one warranting an individual description.

Deer tick,
Ixodes dammini.

Sarcoptic mange, or scabies, is one of the itchiest conditions that affects dogs. The microscopic *Sarcoptes* mites burrow into the superficial layers of the skin and can drive dogs crazy with itchiness. They are also communicable to people, although they can't complete their reproductive cycle on people. In addition to being tiny, the mites also are often difficult to find when trying to make a diagnosis. Skin scrapings from multiple areas are examined microscopically but, even then, sometimes the mites cannot be found.

entire head and mouthparts, which may be deeply embedded in the skin. This is best accomplished with forceps designed especially for this purpose; fingers can be used but should be protected with rubber gloves, plastic wrap or at least a paper towel. The tick should be grasped as closely as possible to the animal's skin and should be pulled upward with steady, even pressure. Do not squeeze, crush or puncture the body of the tick or you risk exposure to any disease carried by that tick. Once the ticks have been removed, the sites of attachment should be disinfected. Your hands should then be washed with soap and water to further minimize risk of contagion. The tick should be disposed of in a container of alcohol or household bleach.

MITES
Mites are tiny arachnid parasites that parasitize the skin of dogs.

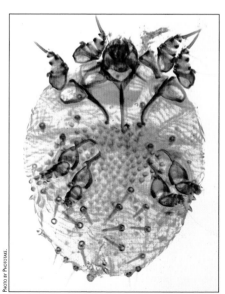

PHOTO BY PHOTOTAKE.

Sarcoptes scabiei,
commonly known as the "itch mite."

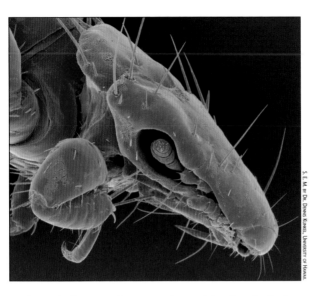

S. E. M. BY DR. DENNIS KUNKEL, UNIVERSITY OF HAWAII

Micrograph of a dog louse, *Heterodoxus spiniger.* **Female lice attach their eggs to the hairs of the dog. As the eggs hatch, the larval lice bite and feed on the blood. Lice can also feed on dead skin and hair. This feeding activity can cause hair loss and skin problems.**

Illustration of *Demodex folliculoram.*

Fortunately, scabies is relatively easy to treat, and there are a variety of products that will successfully kill the mites. Since the mites can't live in the environment for very long without feeding, a complete cure is usually possible within four to eight weeks.

Cheyletiellosis is caused by a relatively large mite, which sometimes can be seen even without a microscope. Often referred to as "walking dandruff," this also causes itching, but not usually as profound as with scabies. While *Cheyletiella* mites can survive somewhat longer in the environment than scabies mites, they too are relatively easy to treat, being responsive to not only the medications used to treat scabies but also often to flea-control products.

Otodectes cynotis is the canine ear mite and is one of the more common causes of mange, especially in young dogs in shelters or pet stores. That's because the mites are typically present in large numbers and are quickly spread to nearby animals. The mites rarely do much harm but can be difficult to eradicate if the treatment regimen is not comprehensive. While many try to treat the condition with ear drops only, this is the most common cause of treatment failure. Ear drops cause the mites to simply move out of the ears and as far away as possible (usually to the base of the tail) until the insecticide levels in the ears drop to an acceptable level—then it's back to business as usual! The successful treatment of ear mites requires treating all animals in the household with a systemic insecticide, such as selamectin, or a combination of miticidal ear drops combined with whole-body flea-control preparations.

Demodicosis, sometimes referred to as red mange, can be one of the most difficult forms of mange to treat. Part of the problem has to do with the fact that the mites live in the hair follicles and they are relatively well shielded from topical and systemic products. The main issue, however, is that demodectic mange typically results only when there is some underlying process interfering with the dog's immune system.

ILLUSTRATION BY PHOTOTAKE

Since *Demodex* mites are normal residents of the skin of mammals, including humans, there is usually a mite population explosion only when the immune system fails to keep the number of mites in check. In young animals, the immune deficit may be transient or may reflect an actual inherited immune problem. In older animals, demodicosis is usually seen only when there is another disease hampering the immune system, such as diabetes, cancer, thyroid problems or the use of immune-suppressing drugs. Accordingly, treatment involves not only trying to kill the mange mites but also discerning what is interfering with immune function and correcting it if possible.

Chiggers represent several different species of mite that don't parasitize dogs specifically, but do latch on to passersby and can cause irritation. The problem is most prevalent in wooded areas in the late summer and fall. Treatment is not difficult, as the mites do not complete their life cycle on dogs and are susceptible to a variety of miticidal products.

MOSQUITOES

Mosquitoes have long been known to transmit a variety of diseases to people, as well as just being biting pests during warm weather. They also pose a real risk to pets. Not only do they carry deadly heartworms but recently there also has been much concern over their involvement with West Nile virus. While we can avoid heartworm with the use of preventive medications, there are no such preventives for West Nile virus. The only method of prevention in endemic areas is active mosquito control. Fortunately, most dogs that have been exposed to the virus only developed flu-like symptoms and, to date, there have not been the large number of reported deaths in canines as seen in some other species.

MOSQUITO REPELLENT
Low concentrations of DEET (less than 10%), found in many human mosquito repellents, have been safely used in dogs but, in these concentrations, probably give only about two hours of protection. DEET may be safe in these small concentrations, but since it is not licensed for use on dogs, there is no research proving its safety for dogs. Products containing permethrin give the longest-lasting protection, perhaps two to four weeks. As DEET is not licensed for use on dogs, and both DEET and permethrin can be quite toxic to cats, appropriate care should be exercised. Other products, such as those containing oil of citronella, also have some mosquito-repellent activity, but typically have a relatively short duration of action.

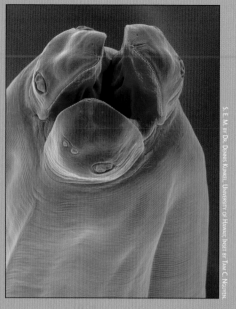

ABOVE: The ascarid roundworm *Toxocara canis*, showing the mouth with three lips.

RIGHT: The hookworm *Ancylostoma caninum* infests the intestines of dogs. INSET: Note the row of teeth at the posterior end, used to anchor the worm to the intestinal wall.

INTERNAL PARASITES: WORMS

ASCARIDS

Ascarids are intestinal roundworms that rarely cause severe disease in dogs. Nonetheless, they are of major public health significance because they can be transferred to people. Sadly, it is children who are most commonly affected by the parasite, probably from inadvertently ingesting ascarid-contaminated soil. In fact, many yards and children's sandboxes contain appreciable numbers of ascarid eggs. So, while ascarids don't bite dogs or latch onto their intestines to suck blood, they do cause some nasty medical conditions in children and are best eradicated from our furry friends. Because pups can start passing ascarid eggs by three weeks of age, most parasite-control programs begin at two weeks of age and are repeated every two weeks until pups are eight weeks old. It is important to realize that bitches can pass ascarids to their pups even if they test negative prior to whelping. Accordingly, bitches are best treated at the same time as the pups.

HOOKWORMS

Unlike ascarids, hookworms do latch onto a dog's intestinal tract and can cause significant loss of blood and protein. Similar to ascarids, hookworms can be transmitted to humans, where they cause a condition known as cutaneous larval migrans. Dogs can become infected either by consuming the infective larvae or by the larvae's penetrating the skin directly. People most often get infected when they are lying on the ground (such as on a beach) and the larvae penetrate the skin. Yes, the larvae can penetrate through a beach blanket. Hookworms are typically susceptible to the same medications used to treat ascarids.

HEARTWORMS

Heartworm disease is caused by the parasite *Dirofilaria immitis* and is seen in dogs around the world. A member of the round-worm group, it is spread between dogs by the bite of an infected mosquito. The

WORM-CONTROL GUIDELINES

- Practice sanitary habits with your dog and home.
- Clean up after your dog and don't let him sniff or eat other dogs' droppings.
- Control insects and fleas in the dog's environment. Fleas, lice, cockroaches, beetles, mice and rats can act as hosts for various worms.
- Prevent dogs from eating uncooked meat, raw poultry and dead animals.
- Keep dogs and children from playing in sand and soil.
- Kennel dogs on cement or gravel; avoid dirt runs.
- Administer heartworm preventives regularly.
- Have your vet examine your dog's stools at your annual visits.
- Select a boarding kennel carefully so as to avoid contamination from other dogs or an unsanitary environment.
- Prevent dogs from roaming. Obey local leash laws.

Ascarid *Rhabditis*

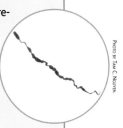

Hookworm *Ancylostoma caninum*

Tapeworm *Dipylidium caninum*

Heartworm *Dirofilaria immitis*

mosquito injects infective larvae into the dog's skin with its bite, and these larvae develop under the skin for a period of time before making their way to the heart. There they develop into adults, which grow and create blockages of the heart, lungs and major blood vessels there. They also start producing offspring (microfilariae), and these microfilariae circulate in the bloodstream, waiting to hitch a ride when the next mosquito bites. Once in the mosquito, the microfilariae develop into infective larvae and the entire process is repeated.

When dogs get infected with heartworm, over time they tend to develop symptoms associated with heart disease, such as coughing, exercise intolerance and potentially many other manifestations. Diagnosis is confirmed by either seeing the microfilariae themselves in blood samples or using immunologic tests (antigen testing) to identify the presence of adult heartworms. Since antigen tests measure the presence of adult heartworms and microfilarial tests measure offspring produced by adults, neither are positive until six to seven months after the initial infection. However, the beginning of damage can occur by fifth-stage larvae as early as three months after infection. Thus it is possible for dogs to be harboring problem-causing larvae for up to three months before either type of test would identify an infection.

The good news is that there are great protocols available for preventing heartworm in dogs. Testing is critical in the process, and it is important to understand the benefits as well as the limitations of such testing. All dogs six months of age or older that have not been on continuous heartworm-preventive medication should be screened with microfilarial or antigen tests. For dogs receiving preventive medication, periodic antigen testing helps assess the

The dog tapeworm *Taenia pisiformis*.

S. E. M. BY DR. DENNIS KUNKEL, UNIVERSITY OF HAWAII.

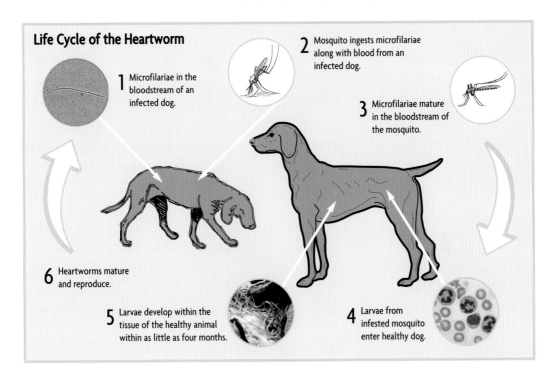

Life Cycle of the Heartworm

1 Microfilariae in the bloodstream of an infected dog.

2 Mosquito ingests microfilariae along with blood from an infected dog.

3 Microfilariae mature in the bloodstream of the mosquito.

4 Larvae from infested mosquito enter healthy dog.

5 Larvae develop within the tissue of the healthy animal within as little as four months.

6 Heartworms mature and reproduce.

effectiveness of the preventives. The American Heartworm Society guidelines suggest that annual retesting may not be necessary when owners have absolutely provided continuous heartworm prevention. Retesting on a two- to three-year interval may be sufficient in these cases. However, your veterinarian will likely have specific guidelines under which heartworm preventives will be prescribed, and many prefer to err on the side of safety and usually retest annually.

It is indeed fortunate that heartworm is relatively easy to prevent, because treatments can be as life-threatening as the disease itself. Treatment requires a two-step process that kills the adult heartworms first and then the microfilariae. Prevention is obviously preferable; this involves a once-monthly oral or topical treatment. The most common oral preventives include ivermectin (not suitable for some breeds), moxidectin and milbemycin oxime; the once-a-month topical drug selamectin provides heartworm protection in addition to flea, tick and other parasite controls.

THE **ABC**S OF
Emergency Care

Abrasions
Clean wound with running water or 3% hydrogen peroxide. Pat dry with gauze and spray with antibiotic. Do not cover.

Animal Bites
Clean area with soap and saline solution or water. Apply pressure to any bleeding area. Apply antibiotic ointment. Identify biting animal and contact the vet.

Antifreeze Poisoning
Induce vomiting and take dog to the vet.

Bee Sting
Remove stinger and apply soothing lotion or cold compress; give antihistamine in proper dosage.

Bleeding
Apply pressure directly to wound with gauze or towel for five to ten minutes. If wound does not stop bleeding, wrap wound with gauze and adhesive tape.

Bloat/Gastric Torsion
Immediately take the dog to the vet or emergency clinic; phone from car. No time to waste.

Burns
Chemical: Bathe dog with water and pet shampoo. Rinse in saline solution. Apply antibiotic ointment.

Acid: Rinse with water. Apply one part baking soda, two parts water to affected area.

Alkali: Rinse with water. Apply one part vinegar, four parts water to affected area.

Electrical: Apply antibiotic ointment. Seek veterinary assistance immediately.

Choking
If the dog is on the verge of collapsing, wedge a solid object, such as the handle of a screwdriver, between molars on one side of mouth to keep mouth open. Pull tongue out. Use long-nosed pliers or fingers to remove foreign object. Do not push the object down the dog's throat. For small or medium dogs, hold dog upside down by hind legs and shake firmly to dislodge foreign object.

Chlorine Ingestion
With clean water, rinse the mouth and eyes. Give dog water to drink; contact the vet.

Constipation
Feed dog 2 tablespoons bran flakes with each meal. Encourage drinking water. Mix 1/4-teaspoon mineral oil in dog's food. Contact vet if persists longer than 24 hours.

Diarrhea
Withhold food for 12 to 24 hours. Feed dog anti-diarrheal with eyedropper. When feeding resumes, feed one part boiled hamburger, one part plain cooked rice, 1/4 to 3/4-cup four times daily. Contact vet if persists longer than 24 hours.

Dog Bite
Snip away hair around puncture wound; clean with 3% hydrogen peroxide; apply tincture of iodine. Identify biting dog and call the vet. If wound appears deep, take the dog to the vet.

Frostbite
Wrap the dog in a heavy blanket. Warm affected area with a warm bath for ten minutes. Red color to skin will return with circulation; if tissues are pale after 20 minutes, contact the vet.

Use a portable, durable container large enough to contain all items.

Heat Stroke

Submerge the dog (up to his muzzle) in cold water; if no response within ten minutes, contact the vet.

Hot Spots

Mix 2 packets Domeboro® with 2 cups water. Saturate cloth with mixture and apply to hot spots for 15–30 minutes. Apply antibiotic ointment. Repeat every six to eight hours.

Poisonous Plants

Wash affected area with soap and water. Cleanse with alcohol. For foxtail/grass, apply antibiotic ointment. Contact vet if plant was ingested.

Rat Poison Ingestion

Induce vomiting. Keep dog calm, maintain dog's normal body temperature (use blanket or heating pad). Get to the vet for antidote.

Shock

Keep the dog calm and warm; call for veterinary assistance.

Snake Bite

If possible, bandage the area and apply pressure. If the area is not conducive to bandaging, use ice to control bleeding. Get immediate help from the vet.

Tick Removal

Apply flea and tick spray directly on tick. Wait one minute. Using tweezers or wearing plastic gloves, grasp the tick's body firmly and pull out. Apply antibiotic ointment.

Vomiting

Restrict water intake; offer a few ice cubes. Withhold food for next meal. Contact vet if vomiting persists longer than 24 hours.

DOG OWNER'S FIRST-AID KIT

- ❏ Gauze bandages/swabs
- ❏ Adhesive and non-adhesive bandages
- ❏ Antibiotic powder
- ❏ Antiseptic wash
- ❏ Hydrogen peroxide 3%
- ❏ Antibiotic ointment
- ❏ Lubricating jelly
- ❏ Rectal thermometer
- ❏ Nylon muzzle
- ❏ Scissors and forceps
- ❏ Eyedropper
- ❏ Syringe
- ❏ Anti-bacterial/fungal solution
- ❏ Saline solution
- ❏ Antihistamine
- ❏ Cotton balls
- ❏ Nail clippers
- ❏ Screwdriver/pen knife
- ❏ Flashlight
- ❏ Emergency phone numbers

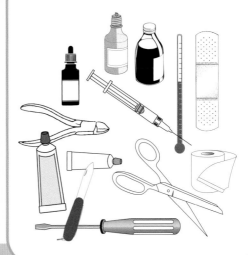

When we bring home a puppy, full of the energy and exuberance that accompanies youth, we hope for a long, happy and fulfilling relationship with the new family member. Even when we adopt an older dog, we look forward to the years of companionship ahead with a new canine friend. However, aging is inevitable for all creatures, and there will come a time when your English Toy Spaniel reaches his senior years and will need special considerations and attention to his care.

WHEN IS MY DOG A "SENIOR"?

In general, pure-bred dogs are considered to have achieved senior status when they reach 75% of their breed's average lifespan, with lifespan being based on size and breed-specific factors. You can make the generalization that 10 to 15 years is a good lifespan for a English Toy Spaniel and thus he is a senior citizen at around 8.

Obviously, the old "seven dog years to one human year" theory is not exact. In puppyhood, a dog's year is actually comparable to more than seven human years, considering the puppy's rapid growth during his first year. The English Toy reaches full height as early as one year, though he takes another year to develop completely. Then, in adulthood, the ratio decreases. Regardless, the more viable rule of thumb is that the larger the dog, the shorter his expected lifespan. Of course, this can vary among individual dogs, with many living longer than expected, which we hope is the case!

WHAT ARE THE SIGNS OF AGING?

By the time your dog has reached his senior years, you will know him very well, so the physical and behavioral changes that accompany aging should be noticeable to you. Humans and dogs share the most obvious physical sign of aging: gray hair! Graying often occurs first on the muzzle and face, around the eyes. Other telltale signs are the dog's overall decrease in activity. Your older dog might be more content to nap and rest, and he may not show the same old enthusiasm when it's time to play in the yard or go for a walk. Other physical signs include significant weight loss or gain; more labored move-ment; skin and coat problems, possibly hair loss; sight and/or hearing problems; changes in toileting habits, perhaps seeming "unhousebroken" at times; and tooth decay, bad breath or other mouth problems.

There are behavioral changes that go along with aging, too. There are numerous causes for behavioral changes. Sometimes a dog's apparent confusion results from a physical change like diminished sight or hearing. If his confusion causes him to be afraid, he may act aggressively or defen-sively. He may sleep more frequently because his daily walks, though shorter now, tire him out. He may begin to experi-ence separation anxiety or, conversely, become less interested in petting and attention.

There also are clinical condi-tions that cause behavioral changes in older dogs. One such condition is known as canine cognitive dysfunction (familiarly known as "old-dog" syndrome). It can be frustrating for an owner whose dog is affected with cogni-tive dysfunction, as it can result in behavioral changes of all types, most seemingly unexplainable. Common changes include the dog's forgetting aspects of the daily routine, such as times to eat, go out for walks, relieve himself and the like. Along the same lines, you may take your dog out

at the regular time for a potty trip and he may have no idea why he is there. Sometimes a placid dog will begin to show aggressive or possessive tendencies or, conversely, a hyperactive dog will start to "mellow out."

Disease also can be the cause of behavioral changes in senior dogs. Hormonal problems (Cushing's disease is common in older dogs), diabetes and thyroid disease can cause increased appetite, which can lead to aggression related to food guard-ing. It's better to be proactive with your senior dog, making more frequent trips to the vet if neces-

SYMPTOMS OF SENILITY

Senility, cognitive dysfunction, mental deterioration, whatever you call it, many dogs experience it as they age. Be aware of changes in your dog, including confusion, in which your dog may fail to recognize you or other family members and/or wander aimlessly around the house; changes in barking patterns or barking for no apparent reason; changes in sleeping habits, such as sleeping during the day and being awake overnight; having toilet accidents in the house or not knowing what to do when you take him out for potty breaks; changes in his temperament and the like. Your vet may prescribe medications or suggest changes you can make around the home and in your routine to make your dog more comfortable.

sary and having bloodwork done to test for the diseases that can commonly befall older dogs.

This is not to say that, as dogs age, they all fall apart physically and become nasty in personality. The aforementioned changes are discussed to alert owners to the things that may happen as their dogs get older. Many hardy dogs remain active and alert well into old age. However, it can be frustrating and heartbreaking for owners to see their beloved dogs change physically and temperamentally. Just know that it's the same English Toy Spaniel under there, and that he still loves you and appreciates your care, which he needs now more than ever.

HOW DO I CARE FOR MY AGING DOG?

Again, every dog is an individual in terms of aging. Your dog might reach the estimated "senior" age for his breed and show no signs of slowing down. However, even if he shows no outward signs of aging, he should begin a senior-care program as determined by the vet. He may not show it, but he's not a pup anymore! By providing him with extra attention to his veterinary care at this age, you will be practicing good preventive medicine, ensuring that the rest of your dog's life will be as long, active, happy and healthy as possible. If you do notice indications of aging, such

---

CAUSES OF CHANGE

Cognitive dysfunction may not be the cause of all changes in your older dog; illness and medication can also affect him. Things like diabetes, Cushing's disease, cancer and brain tumors are serious physical problems but can cause behavioral changes as well. Older dogs are more prone to these conditions, which should not be overlooked as possibilities for your dog's acting not like his "old self." Any significant changes in your senior's behavior are good reasons to take your dog to the vet for a thorough exam.

Your dog's reactions to medication can cause changes as well. The various types of corticosteroids are often cited as affecting a dog's behavior. If your vet prescribes any type of drug, discuss possible side effects before administering the medication to your dog.

---

as graying and/or changes in sleeping, eating or toileting habits, this is a sign to set up a senior-care visit with your vet right away to make sure that these changes are not related to any health problems.

To start, senior dogs should visit the vet twice yearly for exams, routine tests and overall evaluations. Many veterinarians have special screening programs especially for senior dogs that can include a thorough physical exam; blood test to determine complete blood count; serum biochemistry test, which screens for liver, kidney and blood problems as well as cancer; urinalysis; and dental exams. With these tests, it can be determined whether your dog has any health problems; the results also establish a baseline for your pet against which future test results can be compared.

In addition to these tests, your vet may suggest additional testing, including an EKG, tests for glaucoma and other problems of the eye, chest x-rays, screening for tumors, blood pressure test, test for thyroid function and screening for parasites and reassessment of his preventive program. Your vet also will ask you questions about your dog's diet and activity level, what you feed and the amounts that you feed. This information, along with his evaluation of the dog's overall condition, will enable him to suggest proper dietary changes, if needed.

This may seem like quite a work-up for your pet, but veterinarians advise that older dogs need more frequent attention so that any health problems can be detected as early as possible. Serious conditions like kidney disease, heart disease and cancer may not present outward symptoms, or the problem may go undetected if the symptoms are mistaken by owners as just part of the aging process.

There are some conditions more common in elderly dogs that are difficult to ignore. Cognitive dysfunction shares much in common with senility and Alzheimer's disease, and dogs are not immune. Dogs can become confused and/or disoriented, lose their house-training, have abnormal sleep-wake cycles and interact differently with their owners. Be heartened by the fact that, in some ways, there are more treatment options for dogs with cognitive dysfunction than for people with similar conditions. There is good evidence that continued stimulation in the form of games,

RUBDOWN REMEDY

A good remedy for an aching dog is to give him a gentle massage each day or even a few times a day if possible. This can be especially beneficial before your dog gets out of his bed in the morning. Just as in humans, massage can decrease pain in dogs, whether the dog is arthritic or just afflicted by the stiffness that accompanies old age. Gently massage his joints and limbs, as well as petting him on his entire body. This can help his circulation and flexibility and ease any joint or muscle aches. Massaging your dog has benefits for you, too; in fact, just petting our dogs can cause reduced levels of stress and lower our blood pressure. Massage and petting also help you find any previously undetected lumps, bumps or abnormalities. Often these are not visible and only turn up by being felt.

ADAPTING TO AGE

As dogs age and their once-keen senses begin to deteriorate, they can experience stress and confusion. However, dogs are very adaptable, and most can adjust to deficiencies in their sight and hearing. As these processes often deteriorate gradually, the dog makes adjustments gradually, too. Because dogs become so familiar with the layout of their homes and yards, and with their daily routines, they are able to get around even if they cannot see or hear as well. Help your senior dog by keeping things consistent around the house. Keep up with your regular times for walking and potty trips, and do not relocate his crate or rearrange the furniture. Your dog is a very adaptable creature and can make compensation for his diminished ability, but you want to help him along the way and not make changes that will cause him confusion.

play, training and exercise can help to maintain cognitive function. There are also medications (such as seligiline) and antioxidant-fortified senior diets that have been shown to be beneficial.

Cancer is also a condition more common in the elderly. While lung cancer, which is a major killer in humans, is relatively rare in dogs, almost all of the cancers seen in people are also seen in pets. If pets are getting regular physical examinations, cancers are often detected early. There are a variety of cancer therapies available today, and many pets continue to live happy lives with appropriate treatment.

Degenerative joint disease, often referred to as arthritis, is another malady common to both elderly dogs and humans. A lifetime of wear and tear on joints and running around at play eventually takes its toll and results in stiffness and difficulty in getting around. As dogs live longer and healthier lives, it is natural that they should eventually feel some of the effects of aging. Once again, if regular veterinary care has been available, your pet was not carrying extra pounds all those years and wearing those joints out before their time. If your pet was unfortunate enough to inherit hip dysplasia, osteochondritis dissecans or any of the other developmental orthopedic diseases, battling the onset of degenerative

KEEPING SENIORS WARM

The coats of many older dogs become thinner as they age, which makes them more sensitive to cold temperatures and more susceptible to illness. During cold weather, limit time spent outdoors and be extremely cautious with any artificial sources of warmth such as heat lamps, as these can cause severe burns. Your old-timer may need a doggie sweater to wear over his coat.

joint disease was probably a long-standing goal. In any case, there are now many effective remedies for managing degenerative joint disease and a number of remarkable surgeries as well.

Aside from the extra veterinary care, there is much you can do at home to keep your older dog in good condition. The dog's diet is an important factor. If your dog's appetite decreases, he will not be getting the nutrients he needs. He also will lose weight, which is unhealthy for a dog at a proper weight. Conversely, an older dog's metabolism is slower and he usually exercises less, but he should not be allowed to become obese. Obesity in an older dog is especially risky, because extra pounds mean extra stress on the body, increasing his vulnerability to heart disease. Additionally, the extra pounds make it harder for the dog to move about.

You should discuss age-related feeding changes with your vet. For a dog who has lost interest in food, it may be suggested to try some different types of food until you find something new that the dog likes. For an obese dog, a "light"-formula dog food or reducing food portions may be advised, along with exercise appropriate to his physical condition and energy level.

As for exercise, the senior dog should not be allowed to become a "couch potato" despite his old age. He may not be able to handle the morning run, long walks and vigorous games of fetch, but he still needs to get up and get moving. Keep up with your daily walks, but keep the distances shorter and let your dog set the pace. If he gets to the point where he's not up for walks, let him stroll around the yard. On the other hand, many dogs remain very active in their senior years, so base changes to the exercise program on your own individual dog and what he's capable of. Don't worry, your English Toy Spaniel will let you know when it's time to rest.

Keep up with your grooming routine as you always have. Be extra diligent about checking the skin and coat for problems. Older dogs can experience thinning coats as a normal aging process, but they can also lose hair as a result of medical problems. Some thinning is normal, but patches of baldness or the loss of significant amounts of hair is not.

Hopefully, you've been regular with brushing your dog's teeth throughout his life. Healthy teeth directly affect overall good health. We already know that bacteria from gum infections can enter the dog's body through the damaged gums and travel to the organs. At a stage in life when his organs don't function as well as they used to, you don't want anything to put additional strain on them. Clean teeth also contribute to a healthy immune system. Offering the dental-type chews in addition to toothbrushing can help, as they remove plaque and tartar as the dog chews.

Along with the same good care you've given him all of his life, pay a little extra attention to your dog in his senior years and

WHAT A RELIEF!

Much like young puppies, older dogs do not have as much control over their excretory functions as they do as non-seniors. Their muscle control fades and, as such, they cannot "hold it" for as long as they used to. This is easily remedied by additional trips outside. If your dog's sight is failing, have the yard well lit at night and/or lead him to his relief site on lead. Incontinence should be discussed with your vet.

keep up with twice-yearly trips to the vet. The sooner a problem is uncovered, the greater the chances of a full recovery.

SAYING GOODBYE

While you can help your dog live as long a life as possible, you can't help him live forever. A dog's lifespan is short when compared to that of a human, so it is inevitable that pet owners will experience loss. To many, losing a beloved dog is like losing a family member. Our dogs are part of our lives every day; they are our true loyal friends and always seem to know when it's time to comfort us, to celebrate with us or to just provide the company of a caring friend. Even when we know that our dog is nearing his final days, we can never quite prepare for his being gone.

Many dogs live out long lives and simply die of old age. Others unfortunately are taken suddenly by illness or accident, and still others find their senior years compromised by disease and physical problems. In some of these cases, owners find themselves having to make difficult decisions.

EUTHANASIA

When the end comes for a beloved pet, it is a very difficult time for the owners. This time is made even more difficult when the owners are faced with making a choice regarding euthanasia, more commonly known as having a very sick or very aged dog "put to sleep" or "put down."

Veterinary euthanasia can be defined as the act of ending the life of an animal suffering from a terminal illness or an incurable condition; the word "euthanasia" has its roots in Greek, meaning "good death." Euthanasia is usually accomplished by injection or other medical means that do not cause pain to the animal. The pet is injected with a concentrated dose of anesthesia, causing unconsciousness within a few seconds and death soon after. This process is painless for the dog; the only discomfort he may feel is the prick of the needle, the same as he would with any other injection.

The decision of whether or not to euthanize is undoubtedly the hardest that owners have to make regarding their pets. It is a very emotional decision, yet it requires much clear thinking, discussion with the vet and, of course, discussion with all family members. During this time, owners will experience many different feelings: guilt, sadness, possibly anger over having to make this type of decision. Many times, it is hard to actually come to a decision, thinking that maybe the dog will miraculously recover or that maybe he will succumb to

ACCIDENT ALERT!
Just as we puppy-proof our homes for the new member of the family, we must accident-proof our homes for the older dog. You want to create a safe environment in which the senior dog can get around easily and comfortably, with no dangers. A dog that slips and falls in old age is much more prone to injury than an adult, making accident prevention even more important. Likewise, dogs are more prone to falls in old age, as they do not have the same balance and coordination that they once had. Throw rugs on hardwood floors are slippery and pose a risk; even a throw rug on a carpeted surface can be an obstacle for the senior dog. Consider putting down non-slip surfaces or confining your dog to carpeted rooms only.

his illness, making the decision no longer necessary.

When faced with the decision to euthanize, you must take many things into consideration; first and foremost, what is best for your dog? Hopefully you have a good relationship with a vet whose medical opinion you trust and with whom you can discuss your decision openly and honestly. Remember that good vets are animal lovers, too, and want the best for their patients. Your vet should talk to you about your dog's condition and the reality of what the rest of his days

MEMORIALIZING YOUR PET

Whether and how you choose to memorialize your pet is completely up to you. Some owners feel that this helps their healing process by allowing them some closure. Likewise, some owners feel that memorialization is a meaningful way to acknowledge their departed pets. Some owners opt to bury their deceased pets in their own yards, using special stones, flowers or trees to mark the sites. Others opt for the services of a pet cemetery, in which many of the privileges available for humans, such as funeral and viewing services, caskets and gravestones, are available for pets. Cremation is an option, either individual or communal. Owners then can opt to have their dogs' ashes buried, scattered or kept in an urn as a memorial. Your vet will likely know of the services available in your locality and can help you make arrangements if you choose one of these options.

things to think about include the current quality of your pet's life, whether he is constantly ill and/or in pain, whether there are things you can do to give him a comfortable life even if he has an incurable condition, whether you've explored all treatment problems, whether you've discussed the behavioral aspects of your pet's problems with an expert and whether you've thoroughly discussed with the vet your dog's prognosis and the likelihood of his ever again enjoying a normal life.

Of course, the aforementioned considerations present just some of the things that you will need to think about. You will have many questions and concerns of your own. Never feel pressured; take time to make a decision with which you will be comfortable.

If you've come to the decision that euthanasia is the right choice for your pet, there are a few further, equally heartrending, choices to make. Do you or another family member want to be present with your dog during the procedure? How will you say goodbye? Should you arrange for someone to accompany you to the vet for support so that you don't have to drive in a state of grief? Again, your emotions will be running high during this very difficult time, so think your decisions through clearly and rely on the support of family and friends.

will be like; will he be able to live out his days relatively comfortably or will the rest of his life be filled with pain? Many feel that euthanasia is the way to mercifully end a pet's suffering.

You have many factors to consider. Of course, you will speak with your vet and will involve all members of the family in each step of the decision-making process. Some of the

ENGLISH TOY SPANIEL

Is dog showing in your blood? Are you excited by the idea of gaiting your handsome English Toy Spaniel around the ring to the thunderous applause of an enthusiastic audience? Are you certain that your beloved English Toy Spaniel is flawless? You are not alone! Every loving owner thinks that his dog has no faults, or too few to mention. No matter how many times an owner reads the breed standard, he cannot find any faults in his aristocratic companion dog. If this sounds like you, and if you are considering entering your English Toy Spaniel in a dog show, here are some basic questions to ask yourself:

- Did you purchase a "show-quality" puppy from the breeder?
- Is your puppy at least six months of age?
- Does the puppy exhibit correct show type for his breed?

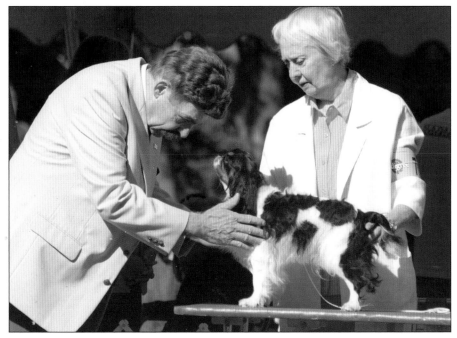

A small breed like the English Toy is examined on a table so the judge can get a closer look.

BEST OF BREED

Best of Variety at Westminster for several years in a row was Ch. Kenjockety Suruca Thomas B, shown with handler Karen Prickett Miller and judge W. Everett Dean, Jr. in 2001.

waggy tail and a pocketful of liver. Even though dog shows can be exciting and enjoyable, the sport of conformation makes great demands on the exhibitors and the dogs. Winning exhibitors live for their dogs, devoting time and money to their dogs' presentation, conditioning and training. Very few novices, even those with good dogs, will find themselves in the winners' circle, though it does happen. Don't be disheartened, though. Every exhibitor began as a novice and worked his way up to the Group ring. It's the "working your way up" part that you must keep in mind.

Assuming that you have purchased a puppy of the correct type and quality for showing, let's begin to examine the world of showing and what's required to get started. Although the entry fee into

- Does your puppy have any disqualifying faults?
- Is your English Toy Spaniel registered with the American Kennel Club?
- How much time do you have to devote to training, grooming, conditioning and exhibiting your dog?
- Do you understand the rules and regulations of a dog show?
- Do you have time to learn how to show your dog properly?
- Do you have the financial resources to invest in showing your dog?
- Will you show the dog yourself or hire a professional handler?
- Do you have a vehicle that can accommodate your weekend trips to the dog shows?

Success in the show ring requires more than a pretty face, a

BECOMING A CHAMPION
An official AKC championship of record requires that a dog accumulate 15 points under 3 different judges, including 2 "majors" under different judges. Points are awarded based on the number of dogs entered into competition, varying from breed to breed and place to place. A win of three, four or five points is considered a "major." The AKC annually assigns a schedule of points to adjust for variations that accompany a breed's popularity and the population of a given area.

a dog show is nominal, there are lots of other hidden costs involved with "finishing" your English Toy Spaniel, that is, making him a champion. Things like equipment, travel, training and conditioning all cost money. A more serious campaign will include fees for a professional handler, boarding, cross-country travel and advertising. Top-winning show dogs can represent a very considerable investment—over $100,000 has been spent in campaigning some dogs. (The investment can be less, of course, for owners who don't use professional handlers.)

Many owners, on the other hand, enter their "average" English Toy Spaniels in dog shows for the fun and enjoyment of it. Dog showing makes an absorbing hobby, with many rewards for dogs and owners alike. If you're having fun, meeting other people who share your interests and enjoying the overall experience, you likely will catch the "bug." Once the dog-show bug bites, its effects can last a lifetime; it's certainly much better than a deer tick! Soon you will be envisioning yourself in the center ring at the Westminster Kennel Club Dog Show in New York City, competing for the prestigious Best in Show cup. This magical dog show is televised annually from Madison Square Garden, and the victorious dog becomes a celebrity overnight.

AKC CONFORMATION SHOWING

GETTING STARTED

Visiting a dog show as a spectator is a great place to start. Pick up the show catalog to find out what time your breed is being shown, who is judging the breed and in which ring the classes will be held. To start, English Toy Spaniels compete against other English Toy Spaniels, and the winner is selected as Best of Breed by the judge. This is the procedure for each breed. At the group level, all of the Best of Breed winners go on to compete for Group One (first place) in their respective groups. For example, all Best of Breed winners in a given group compete against each other; this is done for all seven groups. Finally, all seven group winners go head to head in the ring for the Best in Show award.

What most spectators don't understand is the basic idea of

The English import, Ch. Chacombe Fabian, was Best of Variety at Westminster in 2000, handled by Karen Prickett Miller under judge Frank Sabella.

conformation. A dog show is often referred to as a "conformation" show. This means that the judge should decide how each dog stacks up (conforms) to the breed standard for his given breed: how well does this English Toy Spaniel conform to the ideal representative detailed in the standard? Ideally, this is what happens. In reality, however, this ideal often gets slighted as the judge compares English Toy Spaniel #1 to English Toy Spaniel #2. Again, the ideal is that each dog is judged based on his merits in comparison to his breed standard, not in comparison to the other dogs in the ring. It is easier for judges to compare dogs of the same breed to decide which they think is the better specimen; in the Group and Best in Show

Ch. Cheri-A Lady Isabella Smokey Valley, Best of Variety at Westminster 2001 under judge W. Everett Dean, Jr.

ring, however, it is very difficult to compare one breed to another, like apples to oranges. Thus the dog's conformation to the breed standard—not to mention advertising dollars and good handling—is essential to success in conformation shows. The dog described in the standard (the standard for each AKC breed is written and approved by the breed's national parent club and then submitted to the AKC for approval) is the perfect dog of that breed, and breeders keep their eye on the standard when they choose which dogs to breed, hoping to get closer and closer to the ideal with each litter.

Another good first step for the novice is to join a dog club. You will be astonished by the many and different kinds of dog clubs in the country, with about 5,000 clubs holding events every year. Most clubs require that prospective new members present two letters of recommendation from existing members. Perhaps you've made some friends visiting a show held by a particular club and you would like to join that club. Dog clubs may specialize in a single breed, like the Camino Real English Toy Spaniel Club in California, or in a specific pursuit,

Best of Variety at Westminster in 2002, Ch. Eli-Fran's Sir William with judge Mrs. Barbara Alderman.

such as obedience, tracking or agility. There are all-breed clubs for all dog enthusiasts; they sponsor special training days, seminars on topics like grooming or handling or lectures on breeding or canine genetics. There are also clubs that specialize in certain types of dogs, like herding dogs, hunting dogs, companion dogs, etc.

A parent club is the national organization, sanctioned by the AKC, which promotes and safeguards its breed in the country. The English Toy Spaniel Club of America can be contacted on the Internet at www.etsca.org. The parent club holds an annual national specialty show, usually in a different city each year, in which many of the country's top dogs, handlers and breeders gather to compete. At a specialty

MEET THE AKC

The American Kennel Club is the main governing body of the dog sport in the United States. Founded in 1884, the AKC consists of 500 or more independent dog clubs plus 4,500 affiliated clubs, all of which follow the AKC rules and regulations. Additionally, the AKC maintains a registry for pure-bred dogs in the US and works to preserve the integrity of the sport and its continuation in the country. Over 1,000,000 dogs are registered each year, representing about 150 recognized breeds. There are over 15,000 competitive events held annually for which over 2,000,000 dogs enter to participate. Dogs compete to earn over 40 different titles, from Champion to Companion Dog to Master Agility Champion.

The multiple Best-in-Show-winning Ch. Loujon Backroad Adventure, shown winning at Detroit Kennel Club in 2004 under judge Dr. Samuel Draper, handled by Karen Prickett Miller.

show, only members of a single breed are invited to participate. There are also group specialties, in which all members of a group are invited. For more information about dog clubs in your area, contact the AKC at www.akc.org on the Internet or write them at their Raleigh, NC address.

OTHER TYPES OF COMPETITION

In addition to conformation shows, the AKC holds a variety of other competitive events. Obedience trials, agility trials and tracking tests are open to all breeds, while hunting tests, field trials, lure coursing, herding tests and trials, earthdog tests and coonhound events are limited to specific breeds or groups of breeds. The Junior Showmanship Program is offered to aspiring young handlers and their dogs, and the Canine Good Citizen® Program is an all-around good-behavior test open to all dogs, pure-bred and mixed.

OBEDIENCE TRIALS

Mrs. Helen Whitehouse Walker, a Standard Poodle fancier, can be credited with introducing obedience trials to the United States. In the 1930s she designed a series of exercises based on those of the Associated Sheep, Police, Army Dog Society of Great Britain. These exercises were intended to evaluate the working relationship between dog and owner. Since those early days of the sport in the US, obedience trials have grown more and more popular, and now more than 2,000 trials each year attract over 100,000 dogs and their owners. Any dog registered with the AKC, regardless of neutering or other disqualifications that would preclude entry in conformation competition, can participate in obedience trials.

There are three levels of difficulty in obedience competition. The first (and easiest) level is the Novice, in which dogs can earn the Companion Dog (CD) title. The intermediate level is the Open level, in which the Companion Dog Excellent (CDX) title is awarded. The advanced level is the Utility level, in which dogs compete for the Utility Dog (UD) title. Classes at each level are further divided into "A" and "B," with "A" for beginners and "B" for those with more experience. In order to win a title at a given level, a dog must earn three "legs." A "leg" is accomplished when a dog scores 170 or higher (200 is a perfect score). The scor-

FOR MORE INFORMATION...
For reliable up-to-date information about registration, dog shows and other canine competitions, contact one of the national registries by mail or via the Internet.
American Kennel Club
5580 Centerview Dr., Raleigh, NC 27606-3390
www.akc.org

United Kennel Club
100 E. Kilgore Road, Kalamazoo, MI 49002
www.ukcdogs.com

Canadian Kennel Club
89 Skyway Ave., Suite 100, Etobicoke, Ontario
M9W 6R4, Canada
www.ckc.ca

The Kennel Club
1-5 Clarges St., Piccadilly, London
W1Y 8AB, UK
www.the-kennel-club.org.uk

ing system gets a little trickier when you understand that a dog must score more than 50% of the points available for each exercise in order to actually earn the points. Available points for each exercise range between 20 and 40.

A dog must complete different exercises at each level of obedience. The Novice exercises are the easiest, with the Open and finally the Utility levels progressing in difficulty. Examples of Novice exercises are on- and off-lead heeling, a figure-8 pattern, performing a recall (or come), long sit and long down and standing for examination. In the Open level, the Novice-level exercises are required again, but this time without a leash and for longer durations. In addition, the dog must clear a broad jump, retrieve over a jump and drop on recall. In the Utility level, the exercises are quite difficult, including executing basic commands based on hand signals, following a complex heeling pattern, locating articles based on scent discrimination and completing jumps at the handler's direction.

Once he's earned the UD title, a dog can go on to win the prestigious title of Utility Dog Excellent (UDX) by winning "legs" in ten shows. Additionally, Utility Dogs who win "legs" in Open B and Utility B earn points toward the lofty title of Obedience Trial Champion (OTCh.). Established in 1977 by the AKC, this title requires a dog to earn 100 points as well as three first places in a combination of Open B and Utility B classes under three different judges. The "brass ring" of obedience competition is the AKC's National Obedience Invitational. This is an exclusive competition for only the cream of the obedience crop. In order to qualify for the invitational, a dog must be ranked in either the top 25 all-breeds in obedience or in the top 3 for his breed in obedience. The title at stake here is that of National Obedience Champion (NOC).

RALLY OBEDIENCE

In 2005 the AKC began a new program called rally obedience, and soon this exciting obedience spin-off began sweeping the US. This is a less formal activity yet titles are awarded. There are four levels of competition: Novice, Advanced, Excellent and Advanced/Excellent. The dog and handler do a series of exercises designated by the judge and are timed. Faster and more accurate perfomances are desirable, though each team must work at its own pace. Signs are set up around the ring to indicate which exercise (or combination of exercises) is required. Working closely around

SEAL OF EXCELLENCE

The show ring is the testing ground for a breeder's program. A championship on a dog signifies that three qualified judges have placed their seal of approval on a dog. Only dogs that have earned their championships should be considered for breeding purposes. Striving to improve the breed and reproduce sound, typical examples of the breed, breeders must breed only the best. No breeder breeds only for pet homes; they strive for the top. The goal of every program must be to better the breed, and every responsible breeder wants the prestige of producing Best in Show winners.

the course, the team heels from one sign to the next, performing the various exercises. The judge chooses a series of 10 to 20 exercises out of a total of 50, which vary in difficulty.

The handlers are encouraged to talk to their dog as they work

Best in Show at the Great Lakes Toy Club of Southeastern Michigan in 2005 under judge Mrs. Jacqueline L. Stacy was Ch. Beauprix Baritone.

CANINE GOOD CITIZEN® PROGRAM

Have you ever considered getting your dog "certified"? The AKC's Canine Good Citizen® Program affords your dog just that opportunity. Your dog shows that he is a well-behaved canine citizen, using the basic training and good manners you have taught him, by taking a series of ten tests that illustrate that he can behave properly at home, in a public place and around other dogs. The tests are administered by participating dog clubs, colleges, 4-H clubs, Scouts and other community groups and are open to all pure-bred and mixed-breed dogs. Upon passing the ten tests, the suffix CGC is then applied to your dog's name.

The ten tests are: 1. Accepting a friendly stranger; 2. Sitting politely for petting; 3. Appearance and grooming; 4. Walking on a lead; 5. Walking through a group of people; 6. Sit, down and stay on command; 7. Coming when called; 8. Meeting another dog; 9. Calm reaction to distractions; 10. Separation from owner.

through the course. The judge evaluates each team on how well it executes one continuous performance over the whole course. The team works on its own as soon as the judge gives the order to begin. Handlers develop their own style in working with their dogs, using a combination of body language and hand signals as well as verbal commands.

The dogs love this and it shows by their animation and energy. Many of the dogs who participate in obedience or agility also do well in rally. While most of the first rally titles have gone to seasoned obedience dogs, it's encouraging that some newcomers have also earned awards. Rally is a good way for a begin-

Best in Show at Rogue Valley Kennel Club in 2005, Ch. Cheri A Wingo Lord Marque. The judge was Arley D. Hussin.

jumps, tires, the dog walk, weave poles, pipe tunnels, collapsed tunnels and more. While working his way through the course, the dog must keep one eye and ear on the handler and the rest of his body on the course. The handler runs along with the dog, giving verbal and hand signals to guide the dog through the course.

The first organization to promote agility trials in the US was the United States Dog Agility Association, Inc. (USDAA). Established in 1986, the USDAA sparked the formation of many member clubs around the country. To participate in USDAA trials, dogs must be at least 18 months of age. The USDAA and AKC both offer titles to winning dogs, although the exercises and requirements of the two organizations differ.

ner to start out in obedience. We hope that it will become a stepping stone to the obedience world, and we will see many more dogs and owners coming into the ring.

AGILITY TRIALS

Agility trials became sanctioned by the AKC in August 1994, when the first licensed agility trials were held. Since that time, agility certainly has grown in popularity by leaps and bounds, literally! The AKC allows all registered breeds (including Miscellaneous Class breeds) to participate, providing the dog is 12 months of age or older. Agility is designed so that the handler demonstrates how well the dog can work at his side. The handler directs his dog through, over, under and around an obstacle course that includes

Agility trials are a great way to keep your dog active, and they will keep you running, too! You should join a local agility club to learn more about the sport. These clubs offer sessions in which you can introduce your dog to the various obstacles as well as training classes to prepare him for competition. In no time, your dog will be climbing A-frames, crossing the dog walk and flying over hurdles, all with you right beside him. Your heart will leap every time your dog jumps through the hoop—and you'll be having just as much (if not more) fun!

BEHAVIOR OF YOUR

ENGLISH TOY SPANIEL

You chose your dog because something clicked the minute you set eyes on him. Or perhaps it seemed that the dog selected you and that's what clinched the deal. Either way, you are now investing time and money in this dog, a true pal and an outstanding member of the family. Everything about him is perfect—well, almost perfect. Remember, he is a dog! For that matter, how does he think *you're* doing?

UNDERSTANDING THE CANINE MINDSET

For starters, you and your dog are on different wavelengths. Your dog is similar to a toddler in that both live in the present tense only. A dog's view of life is based primarily on cause and effect, which is similar to the old saying, "Nothing teaches a youngster to hang on like falling off the swing."

Your dog makes connections based on the fact that he lives in the present, so when he is doing something and you interrupt to dispense praise or a correction, a connection, positive or negative, is made. To the dog, that's like one plus one equals two! In the same sense, it's also easy to see that

when your timing is off, you will cause an incorrect connection. The one-plus-one way of thinking is why you must never scold a dog for behavior that took place an hour, 15 minutes or even 5 seconds ago. But it is also why, when your timing is perfect, you can teach him to do all kinds of wonderful things—as soon as he has made that essential connection. What helps the process is his desire to please you and to have your approval.

There are behaviors we admire in dogs, such as friendliness and obedience, as well as those behaviors that cause problems to a varying degree. The dog owner who encounters minor behavioral problems is wise to solve them promptly or get professional help. Bad behaviors are not corrected by repeatedly shouting "No" or getting angry with the dog. Only the giving of praise and approval for good behavior lets your dog understand right from wrong. The longer a bad behavior is allowed to continue, the harder it is to overcome. A responsible breeder is often able to help. Each dog is unique, so try not to compare your dog's behavior with your neighbor's dog or the one you had as a child.

Have your veterinarian check the dog to see whether a behavior problem could have a physical cause. An earache or toothache, for example, could be the reason for a dog to snap at you if you were to touch his head when putting on his leash. A sharp correction from you would only increase the behavior. When a physical basis is eliminated and if the problem is not something you understand or can cope with, ask for the name of a behavioral specialist, preferably one who is familiar with the English Toy Spaniel. Be sure to keep the breeder informed of your progress.

Many things, such as environment and inherited traits, form the basic behavior of a dog, just as in humans. You also must factor into his temperament the purpose for which your dog was originally bred. The major obstacle lies in the dog's inability to explain his behavior to us in a way that we understand. The one thing you should not do is to give up and abandon your dog. Somewhere a misunderstanding has occurred but, with help and patient understanding on your part, you should be able to work out the majority of bothersome behaviors.

SEPARATION ANXIETY

Any behaviorist will tell you that separation anxiety is the most

> ### I CAN'T SMILE WITHOUT YOU
> How can you tell whether your dog is suffering from separation anxiety? Not every dog who enjoys a close bond with his owner will suffer from separation anxiety. In actuality, only a small percentage of dogs are affected. Separation anxiety manifests itself in dogs older than one year of age and may not occur until the dog is a senior. A number of destructive behaviors are associated with the problem, including scratch marks in front of doorways, bite marks on furniture, drool stains on furniture and flooring and tattered draperies, carpets or cushions. The most reliable sign of separation anxiety is howling and crying when the owner leaves and then barking like mad for extended periods. Affected dogs may also defecate or urinate throughout the home, attempt to escape when the door opens, vocalize excessively and show signs of depression (including loss of appetite, listlessness and lack of activity).

common problem about which pet owners complain. It is also one of the easiest to prevent. Unfortunately, a behaviorist usually is not consulted until the dog is a stressed-out, neurotic mess. At that stage, it is indeed a problem that requires the help of a professional.

Training the puppy to the fact

that people in the house come and go is essential in order to avoid this anxiety. Leaving the puppy in his crate or a confined area while family members go in and out, and stay out for longer and longer periods of time, is the basic way to desensitize the pup to the family's frequent departures. If you are at home most of every day, make it a point to go out for at least an hour or two whenever possible.

How you leave is vital to the dog's reaction. Your dog is no fool. He knows the difference between sweats and business suits, jeans and dresses. He sees

Fortunately for English Toys and their owners, the dogs' small size enables them to go along most anywhere.

you pat your pocket to check for your wallet, open your briefcase, check that you have your cell phone or pick up the car keys. He knows from the hurry of the kids in the morning that they're off to school until afternoon. Lipstick? Aftershave lotion? Lunch boxes? Every move you make registers in his sensory perception and memory. Your puppy knows more about your departures than you do. You can't get away with a thing!

Before you got dressed, you checked the dog's water bowl and his supply of long-lasting chew toys, and turned the radio on low.

EXIT STAGE LEFT

Your dog studies your every move. He knows that before you leave the house you gather a bunch of stuff, put on your coat and shake your keys. His anxiety emerges at the first sight of seeing you begin your "exit routine." If your dog suffers from separation anxiety, you should rethink your exit. Mix up your routine and include your dog in some of the tasks. Play a short game of fetch, reward the dog for correct responses to a couple of commands, present him with a safe toy and give him a treat before you leave the house. If the dog is exercised, content and focused on something other than your exit, he may learn to adapt better to your absence.

You will leave him in what he considers his "safe" area, not with total freedom of the house. If you've invested in child safety gates, you can be reasonably sure that he'll remain in the designated area. Don't give him access to a window where he can watch you leave the house. If you're leaving for an hour or two, just put him into his crate with a safe toy.

Now comes the test! You are ready to walk out the door. Do not give your Charlie a big hug and a fond farewell. Do not drag out a long goodbye. Those are the very things that jump-start separation anxiety. Toss a biscuit into the dog's area, call out "So long, pooch" and close the door. You're gone. The chances are that the dog may bark a couple of times, or maybe whine once or twice, and then settle down to enjoy his biscuit and take a lovely nap, especially if you took him for a nice long walk before leaving. As he grows up, the barks and whines will stop because it's an old routine, so why should he make the effort?

When you first brought home the puppy, the come-and-go routine was intermittent and constant. He was put into his crate with a tiny treat. You left (silently) and returned in 3 minutes, then 5, then 10, then 15, then half an hour, until finally you could leave without a problem and be gone for 2 or 3 hours.

If, at any time in the future, there's a "separation" problem, refresh his memory by going back to that basic training.

Now comes the next most important part—your return. Do not make a big production of coming home. "Hi, poochie" is as grand a greeting as he needs. When you've taken off your hat

THE MACHO DOG

The Venus/Mars differences are found in dogs, too. Males have distinct behaviors that, while seemingly sex-related, are more closely connected to the role of the male as leader. Marking territory by urinating on it is one means that male dogs use to establish their presence. Doing so merely says, "I've been here." Small dogs often attempt to lift their legs higher on the tree than the previous male. While this is natural behavior outdoors on items like telephone poles, fence posts, fire hydrants and most other upright objects, marking indoors is totally unacceptable. Treat it as you would a house-training accident and clean thoroughly to eradicate the scent. Another behavior often seen in the macho male, mounting is a dominance display. Neutering the dog before six months of age helps to deter this behavior. You can discourage him from mounting by catching the dog as he's about to mount you, stepping quickly aside and saying "Off!"

and coat, tossed your briefcase on the hall table and glanced at the mail, and the dog has settled down from the excitement of seeing you "in person" from his confined area, then go and give him a warm, friendly greeting. A potty trip is needed and a walk would be appreciated, since he's been such a good dog.

MATTERS OF SEX

For whatever reasons, real or imagined, most people tend to have a preference in choosing between a male and female puppy. Some, but not all, of the undesirable traits attributed to the sex of the dog can be suppressed by early spaying or neutering. The major advantage, of course, is that a neutered male or a spayed female will not be adding to the overpopulation of dogs.

An unaltered male will mark territory by lifting his leg every-where, leaving a few drops of urine indoors on your furniture and appliances, and outside on everything he passes. It is difficult to catch him in the act, because he leaves only a few drops each time, but it is very hard to elimi-nate the odor. Thus the cycle begins, because the odor will entice him to mark that spot again.

If you have bought a bitch with the intention of breeding her, be sure you know what you are getting into. She will go through one or two periods of estrus each year, each cycle lasting about three weeks. During those times she will have to be kept confined to protect your furniture and to protect her from being bred by a male other than the one you have selected. Breeding should never be undertaken to "show the kids the miracle of birth." Bitches can die giving birth, and the puppies may also die. The dam often exhibits what is called "maternal aggression" after the pups are born. Her intention is to protect her pups, but in fact she can be extremely vicious. Breeding

UNDERSTANDING HOW YOUR DOG TICKS

Dogs do not run on human emotions like love, guilt or spite. They operate on trust and loyalty, or faithfulness, and those are worthy alternatives to what we call love. Dogs don't understand any human language, but they can learn to make connections if all corrections and praise are immediate. If your dog demolished your rug while you were out, that's not guilt you're seeing, but a reaction to your anger. He doesn't know why you're angry, but he knows the boss isn't happy. Dogs are pack animals. They have always lived in a cooperative society. Your dog retains that pack instinct, requiring a leader. You now have that job and the responsibility that goes along with it.

Chewing is most commonly associated with puppies, but by no means is the urge to chew eliminated as the dog grows. Providing safe chew toys is of equal importance for puppies and adult dogs.

should be left to the experienced breeders, who do so for the betterment of the breed and with much research and planning behind each mating.

Mounting is not unusual in dogs, male or female. Puppies do it to each other and adults do it regardless of sex, because it is not so much a sexual act as it is one of dominance. It becomes very annoying when the dog mounts your legs, the kids or the couch cushions; in these and any other instances of mounting, he should be corrected. Touching sometimes stimulates the dog, so pulling the dog off by his collar or leash, together with a consistent and stern "Off!" command, usually eliminates the behavior.

CHEWING
All puppies chew. All dogs chew. This is a fact of life for canines, and sometimes you may think it's what your dog does best! A pup starts chewing when his first set of teeth erupts and continues throughout the teething period. Chewing gives the pup relief from itchy gums and incoming teeth and, from that time on, he gets great satisfaction out of this normal, somewhat idle, canine activity. Providing safe chew toys is the best way to direct this behavior in an appropriate manner. Chew toys are available in all sizes, textures and flavors, but you must monitor the wear-and-tear inflicted on your pup's toys to be sure that the ones you've chosen are safe and remain in good condition.

Puppies cannot distinguish between a rawhide toy and a nice leather shoe or wallet. It's up to you to keep your possessions away from the dog and to keep your eye on the dog. There's a form of destruction caused by chewing that is not the dog's fault. Let's say you allow him on the sofa. One day he takes a rawhide bone up on the sofa and, in the course of chewing on the bone, takes up a bit of fabric. He continues to chew. Disaster! Now you've learned the lesson: dogs with chew toys have to be either kept off furniture and carpets, carefully supervised or put into their confined areas for chew time.

The wooden legs of furniture are favorite objects for chewing. The first time, tell the dog "Leave it!" (or "No!") and offer him a chew toy as a substitute. But your clever dog may be hiding under the chair and doing some silent destruction, which you may not notice until it's too late. In this case, it's time to try one of the foul-tasting, spray-on products, made specifically to prevent destructive chewing. These products also work to keep the dog away from plants, trash, etc. It's even a good way to stop the dog from "mouthing" or chewing on your hands or the leg of your pants. (Be sure to wash your hands after the mouthing lesson!) A little spray goes a long way.

DIGGING

Digging is another natural and normal doggie behavior. The English Toy rarely exhibits a strong desire to dig, though every dog is an individual. Wild canines dig to bury whatever food they can save for later to eat. (And you thought *we* invented the doggie bag!) Burying bones or toys is a primary cause to dig. Dogs also dig to get at interesting little underground creatures like moles and mice. In the summer, they dig to get down to cool earth. In winter, they dig to get beneath the cold surface to warmer earth.

The solution to the last two is easy because of course your Charlie sleeps indoors in your temperature-controlled home. However, to understand how natural and normal this behavior is you have only to consider the Nordic breeds of sled dog who, at

---

"LEAVE IT"

Watch your puppy like a hawk to be certain it's a toy he's chewing, not your wallet. When you catch him in the act, tell him "Leave it!" and substitute a proper toy. Chewing on anything other than his own safe toys is countered by spraying the desirable (to the dog) object with a foul-tasting product like Bitter Apple and being more diligent in your observations of his chewing habits. When you can't supervise, it's crate time for Fido.

DOGS OF PREY

Chasing small animals is in the blood of many dogs, perhaps most; they think that this is a fun recreational activity (although some are more likely to bring you an undesirable "gift" as a result of the hunt). The good old "Leave it" command works to deter your dog from taking off in pursuit of "prey," but only if taught with the dog on leash for control.

the end of the run, routinely dig a bed for themselves in the snow. It's the nesting instinct. How often have you seen your dog go round and round in circles, pawing at his blanket or bedding before flopping down to sleep?

Domesticated dogs also dig to escape, and that's a lot more dangerous than it is destructive. A dog that digs under the fence is the one that is hit by a car or becomes lost. A good fence to protect a digger should be set 10 to 12 inches below ground level, and every fence needs to be routinely checked for even the smallest openings that can become possible escape routes.

Catching your dog in the act of digging is the easiest way to stop it, because your dog will make the "one-plus-one" connection, but digging is too often a solitary occupation, something the lonely dog does out of boredom. Catch your young

puppy in the act and put a stop to it before you have a yard full of craters. It is more difficult to stop if your dog sees you gardening. If you can dig, why can't he? Because you say so, that's why! Some dogs are excavation experts, and some dogs never dig. However, when it comes to any of these instinctive canine behaviors, never say "never."

BARKING

Here's a big, noisy problem. Telling a dog he must never bark is like telling a child not to speak! Consider how confusing it must be to your dog that you are using your voice (which is your form of barking) to teach him when to bark and when not to! That is precisely the reason not to "bark back" when the dog's barking is annoying you (or your neighbors). Try to understand the scenario from the dog's viewpoint. He barks. You bark. He barks again, you bark again. This "conversation" can go on forever! Luckily English Toy Spaniels are quiet dogs, and few of them would ever be labeled "yappy." The English Toy tends to use his bark more purposefully and makes an alert indoor watchdog.

If you happen to have an English Toy who is "chattier" than most, there are ways to work with him to encourage proper barking. The first time your adorable little puppy said "Yip" or "Yap, you were ecstatic. His first word! You smiled, you told him how smart he was—and you allowed him to do it. So there's that one-plus-one thing again, because he will understand by your happy reaction that "Mr. Alpha loves it when I talk." Ignore his barking in the beginning, and allow it, but don't encourage barking during play. Instead, use the "put a toy in it" method to tone it down. Add a very soft "Quiet" as you hand off the toy. If the barking continues, stand up straight, fold your arms and turn your back on the dog. If he barks, you won't play, and you should follow the same rule for all undesirable behavior during play.

Dogs bark in reaction to sounds and sights. Another dog's bark, a person passing by or even just rustling leaves can set off a barker. If someone coming up your driveway or to your door provokes a barking frenzy, use the saturation method to stop it. Have several friends come and go every three or four minutes over as long a period of time as they can spare (it could take a couple of hours). Attach about a foot of rope to the dog's collar and have very small treats handy. Each time a car pulls up or a person approaches, let the dog bark once (grab the rope if you need to physically restrain him), say "Okay, good dog," give him a treat and make

him sit. "Okay" is the release command. It lets the dog know that he has alerted you and tells him that you are now in charge. That person leaves and the next arrives and so on and so on until everyone—especially the dog—is bored and the barking has stopped. Don't forget to thank your friends. Your neighbors, by the way, may be more than willing to assist you in this parlor game if it means a quiet dog on the block.

Excessive barking outdoors is more difficult to keep in check,

CURES FOR COMMON BOREDOM

Dogs are social animals that need company. Lonely and tied-out dogs bark, hoping that someone will hear them. Prevent this from happening by never tying your dog out in the yard and always giving him the attention that he needs. If you don't, then don't blame the dog. Bored dogs will think up clever ways to overcome their boredom. Digging is a common diversion for a dog left alone outside for too long. If you catch him in the act of "gardening," it requires immediate correction. Keep your dog safe by embedding the fencing a foot or more below ground level to foil a would-be escape artist. Additionally, keep your dog safely occupied by spending time with him in play activity or just quiet time.

especially if he is outside and you are inside. A few warning barks are fine, but use the same method to tell him when enough is enough. You will have to stay outside with him for that bit of training.

There is one more kind of vocalizing which is called "idiot barking" (from idiopathic, meaning of unknown cause). It is usually rhythmic or a timed series of barks. Put a stop to it immediately by calling the dog to come. This form of barking can drive neighbors crazy and commonly occurs when a dog is left alone for too long. He is completely and thoroughly bored! A few new toys or different dog biscuits might be the solution. If he is left alone and no one can get home during the day, a noontime walk with a local dog-sitter would be the perfect solution.

Although they need some time to adjust to each other, cats and dogs can learn to be the best of friends.

DOMINANCE

Dogs are born with dominance skills, meaning that they can be quite clever in trying to get their way. The "follow-me" trot to the cookie jar is an example. The toy dropped in your lap says "Play with me." The leash delivered to you along with an excited look means "Take me for a walk." These are all good-natured dominant behaviors. Ask your dog to sit before agreeing to his request and you'll remain "top dog."

FOOD-RELATED PROBLEMS

We're not talking about eating, diets or nutrition here, we're talking about bad habits. Face it. All dogs are beggars. Food is the motivation for everything we want our dogs to do and, when you combine that with their innate ability to "con" us in order to get their way, it's a wonder there aren't far more obese dogs in the world.

Who can resist the bleeding-heart look that says "I'm starving," or the paw that gently pats your knee and gives you a knowing look, or the whining "please" or even the total body language of a perfect sit beneath the cookie jar. No one who professes to love his dog can turn down the pleas of his clever canine's performances every time. One thing is for sure, though: definitely do not allow begging at the table. Family meals do not include your dog.

Control your Charlie's begging habit by making your dog work for his rewards. Ignore his begging when you can. Utilize the obedience commands you've taught your dog. Use "Off" for the pawing. A sit or even a long down will interrupt the whining. His reward in these situations is definitely not a treat! Casual verbal praise is enough. Be sure all members of the family follow the same rules.

There is a different type of begging that does demand your immediate response and that is the appeal to be let (or taken) outside! Usually that is a quick paw or small whine to get your attention, followed by a race to the door. This type of begging needs your quick attention and approval. Of course, a really smart dog will soon figure out how to cut you off at the pass and direct you to that cookie jar on your way to the door! Some dogs are always one step ahead of us.

Stealing food is a problem only if you are not paying attention. A dog can't steal food that is not within his reach. Leaving your dog in the kitchen with the roast beef on the table is asking for trouble. Nothing idiopathic about this problem, though perhaps a little idiotic! Putting cheese and crackers on the coffee table also requires a watchful eye

to stop the thief in his tracks. The word to use (one word, remember, even if it's two words pronounced as one) is "Leave it!" Instead of preceding it with yet another "No," try using a guttural sound like "Aagh!" That sounds more like a warning growl to the dog and therefore has instant meaning.

Canine thieves are in their element when little kids are carrying cookies in their hands! Your dog will think he's been exceptionally clever if he causes a child to drop a cookie. Bonanza! The easiest solution is to keep dog and children separated at snack time. You must also be sure that the children understand that they must not tease the dog with food—his or theirs. Your dog does not mean to bite the kids, but when he snatches at a tidbit so near the level of his mouth, it can result in an unintended nip.

PANHANDLING POOCHES

If there's one thing at which dogs excel, it is begging. If there's one thing that owners lack, it's the willpower to resist giving in to their canine beggars! If you don't give in to your adorable puppy, he won't grow into an adult dog that's a nuisance. However, give in just once and the dog will forever figure, "maybe this time." Treats are rewards for correct performance, a category into which begging definitely does not fall.

My English Toy Spaniel

PUT YOUR PUPPY'S FIRST PICTURE HERE

Dog's Name _____*Tina*_____

Date _____ Photographer _____